PRAISE FOR *RADICAL PRAYER*

In *Radical Prayer*, Manny Mill engages us with the idea of a catalytic prayer life that can best be described as "radical!" Why? Simply stated, today's complacency is tomorrow's captivity. Accordingly, today's troubled times require replacing religious and comfortable Christianity with a faith narrative infused by a prayer life that connects heaven to earth. Such a prayer life will ignite a radical faith, founded on radical love, and compelled by radical truth that at the end of day will emerge as nothing less than radically beautiful.

DR. SAMUEL RODRIGUEZ
President, National Hispanic Christian Leadership Conference

Weaving the strands of some amazing stories, the teaching of Scripture, and his own profound experience, Manny Mill offers a compelling and insightful call to prayer. The message of this book could change the landscape of the church.

COLIN S. SMITH
Senior pastor, The Orchard Evangelical Free Church
President, Unlocking the Bible

Manny Mill is both bold and humble. His work on the front lines of ministry in America's prisons and with ex-prisoner ministries requires not just boldness and humility, but also radical prayer. Learn from and with Manny as he explores what that type of praying life looks like.

DR. TONY EVANS
Senior pastor, Oak Cliff Bible Fellowship, Dallas

Manny Mill's *Radical Prayer* is a must-read for all of us. Prayer is how we communicate with God, and Manny explains how the great commission is not possible without radical prayer. As God commands, we want to be submissive to His will. *Radical Prayer* is God's handbook to enable us to do His will.

WARDEN BURL CAIN
Louisiana State Penitentiary Angola, LA

This is a special book, though not because of who the author is or what he has accomplished. Instead it is about how the name of God has been honored and hallowed with the words that have been written. In his own transparent way, Manny Mill shares with us his radical journey of prayer resulting in an enriched and transforming relationship with God.

C. WILLIAM POLLARD
Chairman, Fairwyn Investment Company

I have seen firsthand how Manny and Barbara Mill have sought the Lord in prayer. Thanks be to God for the insight of this prayerful and godly couple.

PETER ROSKAM
US Congressman, Illinois

As the president of an organization committed to the daily practice of prayer by our faculty, staff, and students, I am especially grateful for the challenge of *Radical Prayer*. This book is a clarion call for radical intercession at a time urgently needed in our society—powerfully presenting our best hope for cultural transformation.

HUTZ H. HERTZBERG, DMin, PhD
President, Christian Union

Several years ago Chuck Colson insisted that I had to meet Manny and Barbara Mill. As soon as I did, I understood his urgency. Manny and Barbara are people who are regularly, thoughtfully, and wholeheartedly in the presence of Jesus through prayer, and it shows. This worthwhile book reveals to readers how they developed this joyous discipline, and how it has built a passionate heart in them that beats for their Savior and those He came to save.

JIM LISKE
President and CEO, Prison Fellowship

Manny Mill has written a vital reminder for our day on the subject of prayer. There are many good books on prayer. If you read this book, you are radically consumed to breathe every breath of every day to bring glory to our heavenly Father. It is the "why" of the Christian's life and should be the greatest motivator in our daily walk. This is a much-needed message and encouragement for the church today.

BRIAN RHODES
Vice president and chief ministry officer, Awana

With utter transparency, Manny takes us on his tortuous, personal journey to radical prayer, and I was convicted of inadequacies in my own prayer life. His counsel is compelling and liberating, and has resulted in a deeper, refreshed communion with God.

DAVID K. GIESER, MD
Wheaton Eye Clinic, Illinois

Many of us long for a relationship with Christ steeped in the power of prayer. I have watched Manny Mill up close for many years. His passionate, contagious life of truly radical prayer has shaped my understanding and practice of prayer. Now, you too can walk alongside a friend and mentor and catch a vision of a life radically transformed by the power of prayer.

DR. MARK DILLON
Executive Vice president, American Bible Society

Why another book on prayer? Because what Manny Mill shares here is the real deal. His personal journey from complacency to radical prayer is a must-read for anyone sensing they are playing around with prayer. You will be moved and motivated as you read Manny's bold new discipline of life-altering prayer.

HANS FINZEL
President, HDLeaders and bestselling author, *The Top Ten Mistakes Leaders Make* and *Change Is Like a Slinky*

Manny has presented a biblical model for prayer that will bring you into a deeper and more intimate relationship with your heavenly Father. It is there that you will find a greater capacity to love and pray for others. This will change your life forever.

SCOTT FILLINE
CARBS prayer group coordinator

I have known Manny and Barbara for twenty years and can boldly say that they have lived a radical life for Christ. *Radical Prayer* has challenged me to go deeper in my prayer life, fully convinced that God does things when we pray that He does not do when we don't.

DR. JORGE L. VALDES
Entrepreneur and bestselling author, *Coming Clean*

If God has called you to not just seize the day (carpe diem) but seize eternity (carpe aeternitatum) for your children, your students, and your friends (some of whom may be in prison), *Radical Prayer* is a must-read!

DAVID ROTH, EdD
CEO, Christian Heritage Academy, Northfield, IL

Many books have been written by men on prayer, but some books are written by men of prayer, moved by the love of God. *Radical Prayer* is such a book. This book will stir the hearts of God's people to persist in transformational biblical prayer to the hallowing of God's name and for the greater fame of Jesus!

PASTOR MARCO DAVID
Senior pastor, Midwest Bible Church

Much has been written on the subject of prayer. However, Manny Mill writes from the convicting perspective of his own confession. Convincingly, Manny tackles such questions as "Why don't we pray?" and "What is keeping us from prayer?" *Radical Prayer* will explain how love is the remedy that fuels our hearts to pray like never before.

DR. SAMUEL M. HUDDLESTON
Assistant district superintendent, Assemblies of God, Northern California and Nevada
Author, *Five Years to Life*

God has been pursuing us to seek His face since the garden. *Radical Prayer* is coming at a time when the church desperately needs to wake up and seek God's face! This book is an easy to read, yet powerful encouragement for the church to learn how to pray biblically.

JOSEPH S. AGNELLO, attorney
Board of trustees chair, Koinonia® National Ministries

Radical Prayer is a must-read for any believer. It contains complex teaching that is presented in a way that can be easily understood and applied to your own life. It is convicting, captivating, and challenging. The testimonies within are powerful proof that radical prayer truly brings glory to God.

Dr. Chuck Babb, preaching pastor
CrossPointe Fellowship Baptist Church
Elizabethton, TN

Radical Prayer is a clarion call for today's Christians to fully engage in our divine gift of prayer. Using the weight of Scripture and the power of personal testimony, Manny reminds me of my primary purpose on earth—to bring honor to God's holy name in what I say, in what I do, and in how I pray. I now find myself eagerly awaiting God's radical responses to my radical prayers!

Lynnaea Martin
Member of Radical Time Out (RTO) teaching team

Manny Mill's *Radical Prayer* is both primer and dissertation on the life-giving obedience of prayer. His stories from behind the prison gate are instructive in moving toward God's greater reality through prayer. Manny's love for God is contagious. Be ready to catch it.

David Wessner
Executive producer, Thinking Man Films

There's a great need for *Radical Prayer* to awaken America to the need for prayer and repentance.

Mark C. Curran Jr.
Sheriff, Lake County, IL

There seems to be no shortage of preachers in the church, but unfortunately it is rare to find men who are committed to prayer. Manny is one of those men, and this book and his life are a testimony to us all of the power of a radical, biblical, and committed prayer life.

Scott A. Casto
Businessman and entrepreneur

I will never forget the first time I met my dear friend Manny Mill. Ministering together in prison in Tennessee, I was given the honor of escorting Manny throughout the weekend, as we immediately became "cellies." During that time God used Manny to profoundly convict me regarding my prayer life. As our roads continue to intersect along this journey, Manny continues to challenge me regarding the power of prayer. In *Radical Prayer*, the Holy Spirit has inspired Manny to give the reader a clear, concise, very personal and scriptural guide to radical prayer. I find myself more determined than ever to pray and live radically!

JEFF AND HEITH REYNOLDS
Father and son ministry team
LostCreek Ministries
Wise, Virginia

Manny is an extremely passionate, gifted, chosen, and driven leader for Christ. His energy is so infectious that he inspires people to pray. *Radical Prayer* is a book that calls the people of the church back to its roots, to be a house of prayer for all nations. I strongly recommend *Radical Prayer* because it will bless your church, your friends, your family, and you personally.

JERRY W. DOSS
Senior pastor of Abundant Faith Christian Center
Springfield, IL

Part of the genius of this book is that Manny latches so strongly on to two simple ideas: prayer and love. We live in a secular culture that views prayer as a private phenomenon limited to the church or the prayer closet. Manny tells Christians to pray in social relationships to a great God who answers remarkable prayers.

NATHAN BRUMMEL
Administrator at Divine Hope Reformed Bible Seminary

RADICAL PRAYER

THE POWER OF BEING BOLD AND PERSISTENT

by Manny Mill
with Harold Smith
and Barbara Mill

MOODY PUBLISHERS
CHICAGO

Editor: Jim Vincent
Interior design: Ragont Design
Cover design: Thinkpen Design

Library of Congress Cataloging-in-Publication Data

Mill, Manny.
  Radical prayer : the power of being bold and persistent / Manny Mill.
    pages cm
  Includes bibliographical references.
  ISBN 978-0-8024-1346-8
  1. Prayer—Christianity. I. Title.
  BV210.3.M54 2015
  248.3'2—dc23

                                        2015024586

We hope you enjoy this book from Moody Publishers. Our goal is to provide high-quality, thought-provoking books and products that connect truth to your real needs and challenges. For more information on other books and products written and produced from a biblical perspective, go to www.moodypublishers.com or write to:

Moody Publishers
820 N. LaSalle Boulevard
Chicago, IL 60610

1 3 5 7 9 10 8 6 4 2

CONTENTS

Preface

BECOMING PRAYER RADICALS

WHILE MANNY AND HIS WIFE, Barbara, were closeted away at a friend's Wisconsin cabin writing the final chapters of this book, Judy and I were ourselves "sabbating" at the Fuller Theological Seminary guest house in Pasadena, where I was frantically editing each new chapter as it digitally came in from their friend's Midwest retreat.

By week's end, and with the project ever nearer completion, we felt comfortable leaving our own retreat and making our way back to LAX for a return flight home to Chicago. En route to the airport, we decided to take a quick detour before our scheduled departure and see a nearby piece of God's handiwork called Manhattan Beach.

Oceans have a way of expressing God's enormity, His power and limitlessness—even with the sounds of jet engines flying overhead. So not surprisingly,

Judy and I once again fell under the spell of our God's coastline creation (approximately twenty minutes from runway one), walking along the beach's historic pier and watching the waves rhythmically roll in.

But as God would have it on this picture-perfect afternoon, it was another one of His creations—or should I say "new creations"—that really gave us pause.

His name was George. A sinner saved by grace who was determinedly weaving his way through the crowded pier handing out Gospel tracts to anyone interested.

By the looks of his dark, leathered skin, George had probably been doing this style of evangelism for quite some time—but it was clear his enthusiasm was no less dimmed.

Initially, I had walked right past George without giving him a second thought (after all, we did have a plane to eventually catch). But now I felt compelled to turn around and encourage him in his good work.

No sooner had I identified myself as one of Christ's own, than my new friend—or should I say "brother"—greeted me with an embrace and Christian kiss, and then began to pray. And pray.

And pray some more!

George first thanked God for our meeting. He then prayed for my wife and children. Then for safe travel. Then this book. And finally he prayed for all those we both would be coming into contact with later that day.

After about his third or fourth "Amen," George opened his eyes and said to me: "Look around. See how beautiful everything is. See the power of the waves! And to think, prayer is so much more powerful!"

By now I felt as if God Himself had sent George my way to affirm the reason we were doing this book on prayer!

"Prayer is more powerful," George continued, "because it's all about Him. All about our great God!

"People need to understand that the one we pray to is the one who created all this," he said. "It's because they don't know this that they don't pray. It's because they don't know Jesus that their prayers are left unanswered or they look somewhere else.

"But for us who believe," George concluded, "there is nothing more powerful than going to the throne room of God!"

I could only add my own "Amen" to his quick sermon. We embraced again, and I said my good-byes. (Note to self: Send copy of book to George—somewhere on the Manhattan Pier ☺.)

Pulling into LAX, I realized that in my five-minute encounter with George, he had pretty much covered the principal truth connecting everything in this book: namely, that prayer is not selfishly "willing" or wishing something into being (our culture's understanding), but acknowledging—hallowing as Jesus Himself said in Luke 11—the one to whom we owe our very allegiance, our very lives. For His honor and name alone, we can boldly, persistently—radically—bring our requests to God the Father, through Jesus Christ, as led by His Spirit, and confidently wait for His response.

Prayer is about God, not us.

—

It was George's "God focus"—this "hallowing" of God's name—that I'm convinced is most absent in our prayers today. It's most absent even in the prayers of those of us who supposedly know who we're praying to! After all, when it comes to prayer, we generally see it as a "me first" proposition. We know what we want, and we dutifully line up our myriad requests like some kind of cosmic shopping list. God is our storehouse, and we consequently see Him as a good means to our own ends.

The problem with this, of course, is that when it comes to prayer, God is the end Himself! The glorifying, the hallowing of His name—this is why we pray in the first place. Jesus said no less to His questioning disciples in Luke 11. Everything else—our concerns, our requests—are all to be set before the King as opportunities—as means, if you will—for God to give honor and glory to Himself by answering our petitions in ways only He can. Think "exceedingly abundantly" (Eph. 3:20).

That prayer is more about God than about us is a countercultural message desperately needed today!

Such a message breaks through the selfishness that is so much a part of the cultures and societies we live in—even the churches we attend. And it reminds each of us that our lives are not our own (despite what advertisers and financial consultants say); that we are under the direction (as slaves, according to the apostle Paul in Romans) of Someone else who gives good gifts and who answers our prayers in ways that ultimately give Him glory—and not solely satisfy our wants and needs.

Such is the message of Daniel and his three friends.

Taken captive by King Nebuchadnezzar and, as young men, offered all that the attractive and enlightened (by seventh century BCE standards) Babylonian culture could offer (Daniel 1), this faith-filled foursome nevertheless stood firm—on their knees!—seeking God's direction in every situation: from their diet (Daniel 1) to their vocation (Daniel 2), to their worship and ultimate allegiance (Daniel 3 and 6). Their confidence in their God knew no bounds, for they intimately knew the God they served, and understood that their requests were to ultimately make Him known to the doubters and unbelievers around them through their faithfulness. Thus Shadrach, Meshach, and Abednego could answer both the king's demand that they worship the golden image and his threat that they'd be thrown into the fiery furnace if they didn't, with: "Our God whom we serve is able to deliver us from the burning fiery furnace, and He will deliver us from your hand, O king. But if not, be it known to you, O king, that we will not serve your gods, nor will we worship the golden image which you have set up" (Dan. 3:17–18).

Knowing God for who He is meant that Shadrach, Meshach, and Abednego had the further confidence of knowing that however God answered their prayers in this heated moment (and notice their confidence that He would answer!), it was all about His name, His honor, His glory—and not theirs.

Imagine for a moment if we all approached God's throne room with the same conviction and the same sold-out commitment: "Not my will but thine be done!" I'm convinced God's answers would blow our minds! And His answers would keep us wanting more of the God whose name alone is to be hallowed.

—⁂—

I saw that hunger for more of God in both of my parents. And as a result of their insatiable drive for "things above" (Col. 3:1), I witnessed firsthand the second prayer emphasis woven throughout this book—love. Or more specifically, "neighbor love" manifested in and through prayer that ever seeks to hallow God's name.

Prayer was a natural part of Smith life growing up. My earliest childhood memories are of my dad kneeling, most often by his bedside but also by the living room sofa, usually following family devotions.

Then there was Sunday afternoon. After a makeshift lunch (usually coffee and donuts ☺), Dad would go into their minuscule third bedroom (his "office") with a box of 3x5 cards. *good idea to keep track of prayers*

On each card was a name, a phone number, perhaps an address, and a request. A prayer request. Oh, and usually a date—either of when the request itself was made known to him or the last time Dad had heard an update—an answer—on that request.

With door closed and an old rotary phone at the ready (this was long before today's smartphones), Dad would go through the box of cards one by one, praying for each request and, if it had been awhile since an update, calling the person whose number was on the

19

card. He would then write out the new report and pray over that. Or, more often than not, pray with the person over the phone.

That's neighbor love.

By the end of the afternoon, he would reappear—another hours-long audience before the King of kings completed.

My father defined prayer persistence. It was the air he breathed, the water he drank. And when he would tell me or my sis he was praying for us, we knew it wasn't just arrow shots heavenward, but a continual discourse with the triune God whom my father so hallowed.

Prayer not only expanded Dad's vision to reach the lost, but it filled-to-overflowing his capacity to love others—whoever they were, wherever they were, whatever they had done. Serving was second nature to my father—something he did continually in the home, the community, at church, and most every Tuesday night at Jackson Correctional Center in Jackson, Michigan, where he led Bible studies and from which he'd mentor parolees in their readjusting to life "outside."

Loving God naturally resulted in loving all others! And Dad (along with Mom!) was the consummate hugger!

Maybe it was because he was so radical in his prayer life that near the time of his death his hospice bed in that same little "office" became a literal "house of prayer" in his final weeks on earth. Only this time it wasn't Dad praying (his cancer leaving him unconscious more often than not). Rather, the prayer warriors were those from around the county and even the country whose lives had been impacted by Dad's prayers and love and who now wanted to simply spend a few minutes with the man who had walked the talk and had led so many of them to the Savior.

One visiting prayer warrior in particular I'll never forget. He had been a fellow Ford Motor employee years earlier; an African-American man from Florida who had flown up to Detroit specifically to see my father and to pray over him.

He went into Dad's office for about twenty minutes, and when he came out, brushing his tears aside, he started telling me his story.

He told me about the deep hatred he had early in his life for anyone who was white. He then told me about the first time he met my dad.

"He treated me in ways I could have never expected. Like a friend, with respect," this visitor said. "No harsh language!" And he spent time helping me be the best worker possible.

"He showed me love," this man continued. "And he was always quick to point out it was the love of Christ

for him that allowed him to love me—and everyone—
he managed!

"Your dad's love, his prayers, led me to Christ. His
love, his prayers are why I'm here today."

———⁓⁓⁓———

Recall the words of Jesus as He quoted the Great
Commandment and noted another equally important
commandment:

> One of the scribes came up and heard them
> disputing with one another, and seeing that
> he answered them well, asked him, "Which
> commandment is the most important of
> all?" Jesus answered, "The most important is,
> 'Hear, O Israel: The Lord our God, the Lord is
> one. And you shall love the Lord your
> God with all your heart and with all your
> soul and with all your mind and with all your
> strength.' The second is this: 'You shall love
> your neighbor as yourself.' There is no other
> commandment greater than these." (Mark 12:
> 28–31 ESV)

Love for God and love for neighbor are inseparable
in our life in Christ. And they must also be inseparable

<u>in our prayers</u>. Indeed, radical prayer, as Manny so passionately spells out in this book, fulfills the Great Commandment and, in so doing, equips and unleashes individual believers like you and me to slavishly know and serve God as His loving witnesses to this lost world.

Thus our prayer for this book, that from its reading, we would all become prayer "radicals"—<u>linking every praise, every petition to the hallowing of God's name; and seeing every answer to every prayer as a catalyst to take God's love to all those He brings our way.</u>

If God so loved the world, then we can do no less. And would our prayer lives model that daily.

Beginning with my own!

—HAROLD SMITH

Introduction

HYPOCRISY!

Our Father and our God,
Would You send Your Holy Spirit, with great
unction, upon the reader and create in him
or her a fresh, radical, burning desire to be
confident and secure in Christ? Give the reader
a transformed heart that is receptive to Jesus
Christ—not just as the center of his or her life
but as his or her all in all (Eph. 1:23). May the
reader be rooted and grounded in love to be
able to comprehend with all the saints what is
the width and length and depth and height of
the love of Christ which passes knowledge so
that he or she may be filled with Your fullness
(our paraphrase of Ephesians 1:23; 3:17–19).
In Jesus' name, Amen.

ON OCTOBER 7, 2010, seven years after writing *Radical Redemption*, I was having lunch with some ministry partners at a local restaurant when I got the call. The owner came to our table to say the police were on the phone asking to speak with me. The call was to inform me that my dear wife, Barbara, had been involved in a car accident. A few moments earlier, I had seen the fire trucks and an ambulance pass by the restaurant.

Now I was struggling to comprehend that they had been heading to the scene of a crash involving my wife.

A friend drove me to the site, and my anxiety turned to shock when I saw our car turned upright on the driver's side—all four wheels pointing directly at me. Then I was told Barbara was still inside the vehicle. I wanted to rush to free her from the wreckage, but the police chief, a fellow believer in Jesus and a personal friend, restrained me. He assured me they had everything under control. But in that moment, I wasn't so sure they did!

"Manny, I need you to be calm, cool, and collected," the chief said, as he instructed me to stay where I was. Next he declared, "The only thing you *can* do is pray." Those words hit me hard. They pierced my heart. Inside of me, I cried out, *How can I treat God like a paramedic, only calling out to Him when there's an emergency?*

Waves of desperation and hypocrisy overwhelmed me as the chief began to pray. There on the sidewalk, the Spirit of God began exposing my own shallowness toward God—the very one I had supposedly served faithfully and championed tirelessly in ministry for the previous twenty years. *What had happened to the man who once had a vibrant personal prayer life and wrote a book recounting the amazing things God did in his early days as a follower of Christ?*

When Barbara was finally transferred into the ambulance, I was able to go to her. She had suffered a degloving—the forcible and complete tearing away of the middle three fingers of her left hand. Yet to my amazement, her first question to me was, "How is the woman who hit me?"

Here I was, a visible ministry leader and champion for "the least of these," and I was angry—angry that such a trauma should fall upon our family, especially upon Barbara! But my seriously wounded wife was the one who sang hymns of praise to God in her fight to remain conscious during the ninety minutes she was trapped in her car and who was now demonstrating concern for the woman who drove through the red traffic signal.

I was confronted with my hypocrisy! I had preached sermons about loving your neighbor, but Barbara was living it. I could certainly speak the language of grace (with a Cuban accent, of course). But the demonstration of the fruit of grace listed in Galatians 5:22–23—love, joy, peace, patience, kindness, goodness, faithfulness, meekness, and self-control—was lacking.

Over the next seven months, while Barbara recovered from surgery and endured sixty-four wound care and occupational therapy sessions, I too was "going under the knife"—of the Great Physician.

And my life would never be the same.

1

FROM CRISIS TO CONVICTION

God my Father, I have treated You like a
paramedic. Never again. I messed up. Please
forgive me. Revive my heart! I desperately need
Your radical grace to transform and empower
my heart, through Your Holy Spirit, to develop
a fresh, loving disposition that will produce a
permanent and intimate affection for You alone!
In Jesus' name, Amen!

HOW CAN I TREAT GOD like a paramedic, calling out to Him only when there's an emergency?

That was the question that continually filled my thoughts in the weeks following Barbara's crash.

The paramedics and emergency responders who treated Barbara at the scene were amazing. They had provided wonderful care. And our lives were intensely linked to theirs in those initial hours after the crisis.

But since that terrible moment, those eleven dear life savers had become little more than a faded memory. Our "relationship," as it was, had ended.

So was that how I was now treating God? Calling upon Him during emergency situations, yet selfishly content to go my own way the rest of the time? Was my relationship with God built upon me or upon the blood-stained love of Jesus Christ?

Barbara's trauma became my wake-up call! In that terrible moment, God the Father began to methodically expose my spiritual hypocrisy and replace the joylessness that had filled my Christian walk with a greater love for the Savior and a boundless passion for prayer.

He used two experiences shortly after Barbara's crash to "surgically" cut away from my heart those parts that had turned to stone over time—mercifully giving me a heart of flesh (Ezek. 36:26).

The first came at a pastors' conference I typically attended every year. Since it had been only four months since the collision, I debated about leaving Barbara home alone since she was still in the midst of her therapies. But when she saw the theme was "The Powerful Prayer Life of a Praying Pastor," and knowing that I was wrestling with this issue, she told me in no uncertain terms that I needed to attend and promptly registered me for the event.

PASTORS WITHOUT PRAYER LIVES

About two thousand pastors and ministry leaders gathered together for three days. We sang wonderful songs, listened to eloquent speakers lecture about prayer, and heard stories of the prayer lives of those often considered giants of the faith. Yet not once were we ever called to pray! No time was scheduled for corporate prayer. No one encouraged us from the front to consider skipping a meal (which we were obtaining on our own, so there would have been no waste of meals) to pray individually or with others. Yes, we were told there was a prayer room open throughout the conference, as was the custom each year. But the few times I visited the room to pray, only one or two others were present.

During the conference, we were told that 80 percent of evangelical pastors in America do not have a personal, private prayer life. In other words, the people who are getting paid to pray do not pray! And as if to underscore this point, one of the well-known speakers was asked during a question-and-answer session if he prayed with his wife. He confessed he did not!

It was shortly thereafter that the almost prophetic words of two pastors from a previous generation came to mind.

Charles Haddon Spurgeon, a late-nineteenth-century British pastor, wrote:

> Of course the preacher is above all others distinguished as a man of prayer. He prays as an ordinary Christian, else he were a hypocrite.

He prays more than ordinary Christians else he were disqualified for the office he has undertaken. If you as ministers are not very prayerful you are to be pitied. If you become lax in sacred devotion, not only will you need to be pitied but your people also, and the day cometh in which you will be ashamed and confounded.[1]

According to Spurgeon, I was disqualified for my ministry position and was to be pitied. I had become lax in my sacred devotion, so the people to whom I ministered were also to be pitied because I was not loving them because I was not interceding for them.

The prominent American author on prayer E. M. Bounds, who pastored about the same time as Spurgeon, agreed. He wrote,

The thing far above all other things in the equipment of the preacher is prayer. Before everything else, he must be a man who makes a specialty of prayer. A prayerless preacher is a misnomer. He has either missed his calling, or has grievously failed God who called him into the ministry. . . . Preaching the Word is essential; social qualities are not to be underestimated, and education is good; but under and above all else, prayer must be the main plank in the platform of the man who goes forth to preach the unsearchable riches of Christ to a lost and hungry world. The one weak spot in our Church institutions lies just here. Prayer is not regarded as being the primary factor in church life and activity, and other things, good in their places, are made primary.[2]

Instead of returning from the conference refreshed and recharged, I came home deeply burdened not just for myself but for the church in America. I was acutely aware that other ministry leaders were wrestling with the same prayerlessness and joylessness that I was. According to Bounds, we were either men who had missed our callings or men who had grievously failed the one who had called us into ministry. I was certain I had not missed my calling. So that meant I was grievously failing the one who had called me.

FAILING WITH AN F MINUS

I decided to take a spiritual retreat, all by myself, at a friend's cabin. For those of you who know me well, you will understand how radical this decision was. I am often described as being a people person, one who

needs to be around others. My family even teases me
that I cannot go to another part of the house without
taking someone with me! But I was desperate for a real,
lasting change. I committed to God to spend several
days with Him without the distraction of other people,
the Internet, telephone, or television.

This retreat was my second surgical-like experience. In the quiet of that first hour on the first day, I
asked God to evaluate my last twenty years of ministry.
God saw fit to give me not just an **F** but an **F-**; and He
targeted my dismal prayer life as the primary reason.
I was convicted that my prayer life was putrid. Foul
smelling. Stinky. Like the prophet Isaiah, I became totally "undone" before a holy God (Isa. 6:5).

In my prayerlessness, I had betrayed my wife, our
children, and grandchildren. I failed the investors in the
ministry as well as those men and women in prison and
their families for whom I had been called to be a voice
(Prov. 31:8–9). I had neglected the precious bride of
Christ, the church, for whom I had been called to serve.
I had blindly contented myself with what was a luke-
warm ministry. The Holy Spirit revealed to me that
my prayer patterns and purposes were focused on the
human trinity—me, myself, and I—not on the Holy
Trinity of God the Father, God the Son, and God the
Holy Spirit.

Right then and there, after getting the real perspective and picture of the damage a prayerless life causes, I repented—with deep emotional pains—of my hypocrisy and nonexistent prayer life. I cried out to God my Father and adopted David's prayer of repentance from Psalm 51 as my own.

King David (who today would be labeled a rapist and murderer) had to be restored and experience God's forgiveness the same way I did through genuine, godly sorrow. We both needed God's sufficient grace, regardless of the level or severity of our sin. I prayed David's honest confession of sin and call for mercy, which reads, in part:

> Have mercy upon me, O God,
> According to Your lovingkindness;
> According to the multitude of Your tender
>   mercies,
> Blot out my transgressions.
> Wash me thoroughly from my iniquity,
> And cleanse me from my sin.
> For I acknowledge my transgressions,
> And my sin is always before me.
> Against You, You only, have I sinned,
> And done this evil in Your sight—
> That You may be found just when You speak,

And blameless when You judge. . . .
Purge me with hyssop, and I shall be clean;
     wash me, and I shall be whiter than snow.
Make me hear joy and gladness,
That the bones You have broken may rejoice.
Hide Your face from my sins,
And blot out all my iniquities.
Create in me a clean heart, O God,
And renew a steadfast spirit within me. . . .
Restore to me the joy of Your salvation,
And uphold me by Your generous Spirit.
     (Psalm 51:1–4, 7–10, 12)

No sooner did I receive my failing grade than the Holy Spirit gave me not only fresh mercy but a fresh abundance of undeserved grace. After praying Psalm 51 as my own prayer of confession and repentance, I was reassured that although sin has major consequences, God is willing and able to forgive any repentant sinner, regardless of the sin and its gravity.

JEREMIAH'S MESSAGE OF JUDGMENT—AND HOPE

To give me an example of the serious consequences of prayerlessness and of God's great mercy, the Holy Spirit led me to read through Jeremiah.

The prophet Jeremiah was called by God to proclaim a very difficult and direct message: The southern kingdom of Judah would be devastated by the Babylonians as a result of God's divine judgment on them because of their idolatry. Nearly a century before, the northern kingdom of Israel had been destroyed by the Assyrians and the people had been scattered or taken into captivity, also as a result of God's divine judgment. The leaders of the southern kingdom thought that such destruction would never befall them. After all, they had the temple in Jerusalem, the very dwelling place of God!

God, however, saw things differently. In Jeremiah 10:18, He said He was going to throw the people of Judah out of their land and distress them. Why? Verse 21 gives one reason, "For the shepherds have become dull-hearted, and have not sought the Lord; therefor, they shall not prosper, and all their flocks shall be scattered."

This verse reminded me of what I knew about myself and had heard and seen at the pastors' conference. We, the shepherds, were not seeking the Lord. We were not—I was not—praying.

But praise be to our great God; Jeremiah's message is not all about judgment. It is also about God's mercy that brings redemptive and reviving hope.

While Jeremiah is locked up in the king's prison

(because King Zedekiah did not like what Jeremiah was prophesying), the Lord instructs him to purchase some land. This would have seemed like a crazy thing for Jeremiah to do. Why buy land in a place that is about to be overtaken by an enemy and from which you will soon be deported? Yet Jeremiah obeys. He does as God commanded without delay—buys the land and seals the purchase deeds in a safe place. The next thing he does is pray (Jer. 32:16). Unlike the priests—the so-called shepherds of Israel who had become dull-hearted and did not seek the Lord—Jeremiah turns to the Lord for understanding about what he had just done.

The Lord responds to Jeremiah with remarkable, loving devotion, giving him words of great hope that I took personally to heart for myself and for the people that God has called me to serve. He answers Jeremiah with a question (Jer. 32:26–27), which I felt like God was asking me that day: "Behold, I am the Lord, the God of all flesh. Is there anything too hard for Me?" He tells Jeremiah that He will send the Babylonians to drive them out of the land, but one day He will bring them back. Jeremiah 32:38–41 says,

> They shall be My people, and I will be their
> God; then I will give them one heart and one
> way, that they may fear Me forever, for the

good of them and their children after them.
And I will make an everlasting covenant with
them, that I will not turn away from doing
them good; but I will put My fear in their
hearts so that they will not depart from Me.
Yes, I will rejoice over them to do them good,
and I will assuredly plant them in this land,
with all My heart and with all My soul.

Although the present time was very grim, God reminded Jeremiah that He would do His people good.
That good was to cause them to revere Him, to fear
Him in the good sense of the word, so that they would
not depart from Him. This was exactly what He was
doing with me.

INTIMATE FELLOWSHIP WITH GOD MY FATHER

I savored the sweetness of an intimate fellowship
with God my Father, through Jesus Christ, like never
before. It was even greater than when Jesus first found
me and confronted me in Caracas, Venezuela, where I
had been hiding from the FBI and facing fifty-five years
in prison—and then experienced His radical redemption. But now the Holy Spirit was energizing me with
fresh power and giving me a renewed confidence in
the finished redemptive work of Christ. God provided

me with a fresh start in ministry by filling me with the hope of His glory revealed through the person of Jesus Christ. He gave me a new beginning, as He did with King David, the nation of Israel, and the apostle Peter (see John 21:15–19). The Holy Spirit reminded me that God the Father could have fired me at that very moment. There was justifiable cause for my termination. Yet He chose to give me abundant mercy instead. ¡Aleluya!

Jeremiah 33:2–3 are two of the most oft-quoted verses on prayer. We are told that while Jeremiah was still in prison, God spoke to him a second time saying, "Thus says the Lord who made it, the Lord who formed it to establish it (the Lord is His name): 'Call to Me, and I will answer you, and show you great and mighty things, which you do not know.'"

Right then, I called out to God, thanked Him for His mercy in restoring me, and asked Him to show me great and mighty things that I did not know. Because of His great mercy, I now had a renewed personal relationship with Him. No longer would I call upon God as a paramedic, but rather I would call upon Him as my Father.

I genuinely sensed that God gave me an assurance that I would live to see a revival in the church in America and that the revival would begin in the most unlikely of places, America's prisons. He would use "the foolish things of this world [inmates and former inmates, such as me] to shame the wise" (1 Cor. 1:27). As I prayed about such a revival, the proverbial words of William Carey, the man called "the father of modern missions" (and a man who was often at odds with church leadership), came to my mind. While appealing to a group of pastors to join him in missionary work, Carey said, "Expect great things; attempt great things."

That is what I purposed to do, and I knew the first step would be for God to revive me, to change me and my heart.

Later that day, I sat for several hours alongside the river that borders my friend's property. Although I am not typically the kind of person who enjoys spending much time outdoors, especially in February in Wisconsin, I felt drawn by the Holy Spirit to watch the waters flow by and observe the riverbanks. God spoke to me through this part of His creation, bringing to my mind the word "capacity." I cried out to God to give me a greater capacity for prayer, for communing with Him. I opened myself up to be filled with God's pattern for powerful, passionate, and personal prayer. As God created this very section of the earth to have a capacity to hold these river waters—a depth, a width, and a length—so I needed God to give me the capacity to receive, retain, and then respond to His grace as I began a new journey in the discipline of radical, biblical prayer.

2

FROM CONVICTION TO RADICAL CHANGE

*My loving heavenly Father, I plead with You
and I appeal to You, in Jesus' name, to make
my personal, radical, and biblical prayer
life my single aim and life pursuit—all for
the hallowing of Your holy name. Infuse me
with a fresh and burning desire, through
Your Spirit, to go hard after You each
and every day of my life!
In Jesus' name, Amen!*

IMMEDIATELY UPON MY repenting, the Holy Spirit made it clear to me that developing my own personal, biblical prayer life had to become my single aim and life pursuit. This was nonnegotiable—and even more important than the water I drink each day. He told me that preaching His Word, which I had been called to do, would be ineffective without fervent prayer. Even with the best Christian education and sermon preparation techniques, those messages would be powerless without sincere and regular prayer.

E. M. Bounds said as much when he wrote the following in "The Necessity for Praying Men":

The men to whom Jesus Christ committed the fortunes and destiny of His Church were men of prayer. . . . The Apostles allowed no duty, however sacred, to so engage them as to infringe upon their time and prevent them from making prayer the main thing. . . . The seed of God's Word must be saturated in prayer to make it germinate. It grows readier and roots deeper when it is prayer-soaked.[1]

Citing Jesus as our supreme example, Bounds continued:

Jesus Christ was the divinely appointed leader of God's people, and no one thing in His life proves His eminent fitness for that office so fully as His habit of prayer. Nothing is more suggestive of thought than Christ's continual praying, and nothing is more conspicuous about Him than prayer. His campaigns were arranged, His victories gained, in the struggles and communion of His all-night praying. . . . What an inspiration and command to prayer is Christ's life! What a comment on its worth! How He shames our lives by His praying!

I became convicted that from that moment on my emotions and my decisions needed to be driven by Scripture alone; and that prayer must precede my every step. I had taught many the principle of *sola Scriptura*—only the Scriptures—over the years, but I had stopped living it because I had stopped praying it. I knew that in order for me to cultivate a prayer life, my prayers had to be fueled by Scripture. This is what I call radical, biblical prayer.

Radical is from the word meaning "root." My prayer life had to become the root for the whole of my life. *Biblical* means that the Word of God needs to be the soil into which that root must go deep and take hold of its nutrients. I needed to become the man described in Psalm 1, one who meditates on God's Word "day and night . . . like a tree planted by the rivers of water, that brings forth its fruit in its season, whose leaf also shall not wither" (vv. 2–3). The Bible is, after all, the living Word of God. It is 100 percent powerful and fully reliable. It is sufficient for every need. We are not to take it for granted or treat it lightly.

In the very last words that Moses spoke to the children of Israel, he admonished them to set their hearts on the law of God for it was their very life (Deut. 32:45–47). I once heard life defined as *Living In Freedom Every* day. That is the way I wanted to live.

ON THE FLOOR IN PRAYER

There in the cabin, I began to cultivate a new discipline. I literally placed my Bible on the floor in front of me as I knelt to pray. First I read aloud a portion of Scripture to God. Then I started to pray in a threefold manner I later discovered that Martin Luther, one of the great theologians of the Protestant Reformation, had advised someone to follow. The great reformer advised his mentee to select any text from the Bible, then pray it three times: first as a thanksgiving, second as a confession, and third as a petition.

I turned to 2 Chronicles 6 and 7 and read about King Solomon praying to God that his eyes would be open and his ears would be attentive to the prayers that would be offered in the temple Solomon had just constructed. I read about the priests and people rejoicing because of the goodness of the Lord, so I rejoiced aloud about the goodness and mercy I was receiving from God at that very moment. Here was Solomon, a man who had come from a messed-up family, being given the privilege of seeing the glory of the Lord so engulf the temple that the priests could not even enter it (2 Chron. 7:2). As a man who had messed up my own family through my own sinfulness, I recognized I too was being given an opportunity to start anew in ministry. As the people at the temple's dedication, I bowed and remembered their words, "He is good, for His mercy endures forever" (v. 3).

Next, I had to confess to the Lord that I had not humbled myself before Him. I repented of not seeking His face and made a commitment to turn from my prayerlessness (v. 14). Then, I presented my petition to Him: That he would openHis eyes and make His ears attentive to my prayer so that I would know more of His heart (vv. 15–16).

For some time, I continued to kneel and read aloud this Scripture, weeping and praying words of thanksgiving, confession, and petition. As Solomon prayed for God to fill the temple with His presence—His glory— so I prayed that God would fill me with His presence. I soon felt that I was being filled with the same glory that had filled the temple, and I did not want it to stop.

Perhaps that last statement sounds too bold for some of you. It is indeed a bold statement, yet I hope it challenges you to surrender yourself and seek the same "filling." Throw yourself upon the irresistible grace of God so you will be filled with the glory of God through the explosive power of His Spirit. I remind you that the apostle Paul teaches that believers are now the temple of the Holy Spirit (1 Cor. 6:19), and that we are also vessels of mercy prepared for glory and to make known the riches of His glory (Rom. 9:23–24).

Beloved reader, I urge you to take a radical time-out *right now*. Put down *this* book and pick up *the* book, God's Holy Word. Select a text, read it aloud, and then pray it back to your Father in heaven.

Let the Word of God fuel your prayers. Search out what the passage teaches you about our God and praise Him for that. Confess any sin that comes to mind as a result of reading this passage. Then petition God, for yourself and for others, that the Holy Spirit would work the necessary changes in you.

PRAYER WALKING

The changes in my praying led to other changes almost immediately.

My weight was out of control. It was a terrible and visible testimony to my prayerless life. For some time I had been ignoring the warnings about my weight from my dear friends Tom and Wendy Horton, who "just" happened to be personal fitness trainers. We had recently begun to minister together, working with former inmates and occasionally preaching and teaching in county jails and state prisons. There I was telling the guys and gals who were incarcerated that they needed to stop defiling God's temple through their addictions to drugs, alcohol, and pornography, but I could not control my food intake or make time to exercise. I was being a despicable witness for Jesus. The Hortons challenged me that my walk did not match my talk.

On my second day at the cabin, the Holy Spirit commanded me to start walking. He told me to walk in His power and under the authority of Christ Jesus. He promised that He would counsel me and help me with the necessary discipline, motivation, and new habits needed to lose the weight and keep it off.

I knew that if I delayed my obedience, I would miss His blessing. I also realized that this Spirit-directed workout plan would provide me an opportunity to pray. So off I went, walking and praying.

The hard part came when I returned home. It was the middle of February. The weather in Chicagoland at that time of year can be brutal. The nice, cushioned indoor track at the local YMCA was not an option because I was committed to praying while I walked. And for this Cuban, praying meant praying audibly (and, at times, loudly). It also meant praying in Spanish.

Spanish is my first language. I did not learn English until I was almost sixteen and then really only used it in school. In all other areas of my life, Spanish was my primary language until I went to prison in 1986.

Some call your first language your "mother tongue" or "heart language." Although you can become fluent in another language, it is usually in your heart language that you best express yourself. So my "Hallelujah!" is always "¡Aleluya!" During my spiritual retreat, I realized I had stopped praying in Spanish. I wanted to be 1,000 percent transparent with God. I wanted to be able to express my most intimate thoughts with Him. I wanted to come clean. So I made it a point to return to praying in Spanish during my private prayer times.

OUT INTO THE COLD

Barbara realized the significance of my commitment as I bundled up to face the bitter Chicago cold. Although she wanted to tell me it was too cold to walk outside, she also understood there could be serious spiritual consequences if I delayed my obedience.

Little wonder, then, that one of my first prayers was for God to give me the discipline each day to get out and walk regardless of my feelings—or the Chicago weather! I had read somewhere, "Discipline is doing what you know needs to be done, even though you don't want to do it." My first walks were not long, but I began to gradually lengthen and vary my routes through our neighborhood—sometimes with unexpected and even humorous consequences.

For example, my son's high school history teacher once asked him, "Is your dad trying to learn another language? I see him walk by our house almost every day, wearing headphones. I can't really hear what he's saying, but I know he's not speaking English."

Another time, we bumped into a couple at a local restaurant with whom we attended church. While catching up on our families, we learned that their daughter Kristen had just moved into our neighborhood. My wife jokingly said, "That's good. Now Kristen can reassure her neighbors that the man who walks the streets talking to himself really isn't crazy." Kristen's mom got a funny smile on her face. She then proceeded to tell us about the day Kristen had taken a friend to look at the house she and her husband were considering buying. As they stood outside looking over the landscaping, Kristen heard a voice she recognized— mine. She told her mom that she heard me before she saw me and that I was so intent on my walking and praying that I never even noticed her or her friend.

The discipline of prayer walking has helped me lose (and keep off) over eighty pounds. But this transformation is not just for my benefit. It has also given a credibility to the power of God at work in my life and is a testimony to others of what God can do. Now my physical body is in better shape to function for the hallowing of God the Father's holy name and for the loving of my neighbor.

3

CLEARING AWAY DISTRACTIONS

Father, You are my awesome Father. ¡Aleluya!
I never want to dishonor Your holy name
again! I want my body (Your temple), where
You dwell with permanency through Your
Spirit, to hallow Your name with absolute,
visible credibility. Make me more than a
conqueror according to Your Word in
Romans 8:37 in continuing to be disciplined
in my eating and exercising regularly,
so that I may hallow Your holy name.
In Jesus' name, Amen!

SINCE THERE WAS a noticeable change in my physical appearance, people began to ask about my health. I was, after all, at that age when physical challenges begin to arise, and many thought my weight loss might be due to illness. In fact, people were often afraid to ask me directly about all this, so they would pull my wife aside and ask in hushed tones, "Is Manny okay?" There were astonished looks when Barbara would tell them that the weight loss was the result of prayer walking!

In addition to prayer walking, I began to build

other equally critical prayer habits. For example, I began and ended each day by kneeling in prayer—and still do so today. This position is one of reverence, submission, and surrender. And, yes, it is found in the Scriptures. The apostle Paul knelt in prayer (Eph. 3:14), as did Daniel, three times a day (Dan. 6:10). Solomon offered the prayer of dedication for the temple from a posture of kneeling, with his hands spread out toward the heavens (2 Chron. 6:13). If these great men all knelt to pray, then why not I?

I also became intentional about praying with my wife whom I am commanded to love as Christ loves the church. It is also a way I can honor her as a fellow-heir of the grace of life. First Peter 3:7 says if I do this my prayers will not be hindered.

But while I was enjoying a new intimacy with the triune God through private prayer and times with Barbara, I continued to be burdened for others and the prayerlessness I saw around me. I could not shake the experience of spending three days with two thousand pastors and ministry leaders at a conference *on prayer* and yet never praying corporately. If, as we were told (and seemed to be demonstrating ourselves), 80 percent of pastors do not pray, then what did that say about the people in the pews? Where was the sense of urgency? And what was keeping God's people from bold, passionate, persistent, radical prayer?

Certainly it was not from a lack of information about the great needs all around us. For example, the breakdown of the family. What man, woman, or child has not been affected in some way by unfaithfulness or divorce? Or consider the economic burdens weighing down so many of us. Or the rise of senseless crime. Many are affected directly or indirectly by drug and alcohol abuse. The concerns are legion. If these issues alone—not to mention countless others—did not create a sense of urgency in prayer, what could?

OUR FEARS OF PRAYING

What keeps us from being urgent in prayer?

The answer I was led to may surprise you. But it's one my own life pointed to as a major roadblock to effectual praying.

That roadblock? Fear.

Three basic fears block our path to prayer. First, we *fear having our sins exposed.* As I wrote about in my first book, *Radical Redemption*, my life was all about the unholy trinity of me, myself, and I. I had every vice available to me—and there were very few I didn't partake of. I was totally comfortable with my sin. Totally comfortable, that is, until the Spirit grabbed ahold of me while running from US authorities in South America. It was during one particularly momentous phone call with my father back in America that I found myself—sins and all!—suddenly being drawn into the presence of the very one who is holy, holy, holy. His light began to expose the dirt inside me. And it wasn't pretty!

Not surprisingly, such exposure leads to the fear of pain. Spiritual transformation—the uprooting of self and replacing the idol of me, myself, and I with the triune God—is usually painful. Coming into the presence of God for Isaiah involved a vision of an angel touching his unclean lips with a burning coal in order to transform his mouth into a pure vessel that could proclaim the messages of God. Suddenly the very words of our mouths and the meditations of our hearts are not our own but God's. And that can be troubling.

Finally there's fear of losing control. When you seek another's help in shared times of prayer, you give up control and indicate a willingness to do things in ways you have not considered. Coming into the presence of the one who is Almighty God, maker of heaven and earth, means His will and not yours be done! And that can be unsettling.

THE ANSWER TO OUR FEARS

My friends, fear is the roadblock to effectual prayer. But the answer to our fear may surprise you as well. It's not courage. But rather, love. And not just any kind of love, but a specific, supernatural love that the apostle John describes as follows: "There is no fear in love; but perfect love casts out fear, because fear involves torment. But he who fears has not been made perfect in love. We love Him because He first loved us" (1 John 4:18–19).

The perfect love of God is the answer to our fear. For only through the love of God can we enter into a relationship with Him and His beloved Son Jesus, who is the way, the truth, and the life (John 14:6). And it is only with this love that we can overcome the fear of exposed sin, the fear of transformational pain, and the fear of completely surrendering self to the awesome creator Himself.

And who is this awesome God?

+ He is loving and merciful, abounding in goodness and truth (Ex. 34:6).
+ He pardons iniquity and does not retain His anger forever. Why? Because He delights in mercy and will give us truth (Mic. 7:18–20).
+ He "desires all men to be saved [that is love] and to come to the knowledge of truth." He is the one God, and His Son, the God-man Christ Jesus, "gave Himself a ransom for all" (1 Tim. 2:4–6).

This is the love that will conquer every *f*alse evidence which *a*ppears *r*eal—FEAR— that exists.

God the Father's love is real, liberating, transforming, and compelling. Knowing this is essential to overcoming the roadblock of fear and developing a sense of urgency in our prayers.

I observe such urgency whenever I participate with a group of men who meet together for prayer each Saturday. They are serious prayer warriors, demonstrating their love for others by interceding for them early each and every Saturday morning. Our leader announces what Scripture passage will be read and asks someone to pray that God would illumine our minds (1 Cor. 2:14) and open the eyes of our hearts (Eph. 1:18–19) to understand that portion of His Word and to fuel our prayers. After the Scripture is read, we go directly to prayer. As the Holy Spirit leads, men raise their voices like orchestral instruments playing a symphony of praise, confession, and petition before God our Father.

Praise be to our great God! Fear is overcome by God's love.

The Father's great love has been revealed to us in the person of His Son, Jesus Christ, who, though being God Himself, became man in order that He could become the perfect sacrifice required to pay the penalty of our sin and fully and permanently satisfy the wrath of His Father's righteous judgment against us.

EXAMINATION TIME

Beloved reader, I urge you now to take a moment to examine your relationship with this amazing God. Do you believe that only those who trust in Christ can be declared not guilty of treason against the Most High God? Do you believe that because of Christ's death on the cross we can be saved from the slavery of sin, the guilt of sin, and an eternal hell? If not, I implore you to stop right now and take a radical time-out. Reflect on this liberating truth that will free you from self, sin, and hell. Confess with your mouth and believe in your heart that God the Father raised Jesus from the dead (Rom. 10:9–10).

If you do believe, then cry out to God to give you a greater understanding of His great love for you. Let His perfect love drive away the fears that have been hindering your prayers, oppressing you, and stealing your joy. Then begin to pray in the confidence we have in Christ. Our confidence is not in our prayers, it is not even in our faith. Rather, our confidence is in the person of Christ who has opened the way for us to have access to God the Father (Eph. 3:12).

TAKING RISKS: MARCO, ERIC, AND FREDIE

When I think of people whose confidence in Christ overcame their fears, I think of my pastor friend Marco David, his brother Eric, and one of their fellow church elders, Fredie.

For many years, in addition to pastoring, Marco was a Chicago police officer, as was Eric. Not only did these brothers risk their lives in the line of duty, but they spent their off-duty hours back on the streets bringing God glory by proclaiming the good news of Jesus to whoever would listen. Instead of letting their hearts be hardened by what they saw on the job, Marco and Eric embodied the love of Christ that, in turn, created a sense of urgency for proclaiming the gospel, regardless of the consequences.

One day, Eric was doing public ministry in the gang- and drug-infested Humboldt Park neighborhood of Chicago when he spotted nineteen-year-old Fredie walking down the street. Eric had had a previous encounter with Fredie so he approached him again and now began to talk to him about the Lord. Little did he know that in the box Fredie was carrying was an assault rifle—one of the many weapons Fredie supplied to gang members in the neighborhood.

Fredie remembers Eric describing to him in detail the sufferings of Christ and His death on the cross to pay for *his* sins, something he had never heard before. Until that day, his understanding of Christ was limited to what he saw in paintings of Jesus. Eric's words about the amazing love of the cross left a deep impression in Fredie's heart that God would use weeks later.

Fredie was a confused young man. He wanted a change from his life of violence, drugs, and drive-by shootings. Fredie felt he had done so much wrong that he could never be forgiven by God. A gang member since age ten, he had brought so many people into the gang he wondered how he could possibly leave. Could he really change?

Fredie prayed for God to show him who in his gang and life was for him and who was against him. There was not a lot of deep theology in his prayer, but it was an honest cry from his heart. God had ignited in Fredie a spark of faith. Fredie's prayer, in light of the love and hope of the cross, was a distress call like King David's in Psalm 18:6, "In my distress I called upon the Lord, and cried out to my God; He heard my voice from His temple, and my cry came before Him, even to His ears." Fredie needed God in a big way and his distress call was heard by God in a big way!

Over the next few weeks things went from bad to worse. Through a series of events, Fredie began to feel that his friends were not looking out for him. He turned to harder drugs, and became more reckless and out of control. In his confused state, he was hoping that those he thought "had his back" would try to stop him. Instead, they turned their backs on him. Although Fredie did not yet realize it, God was specifically answering his heart's cry to see who was for him and who was against him.

His destructive behavior came to a climax one night while attempting to run over some rival gang bangers with his car. As he made a U-turn and headed in the direction of his rivals, a police patrol spotted him and began a pursuit. Fredie managed to flee from the police and returned home. An overwhelming weight began to fall upon him as he thought about his life and where he was headed. He knew it was just a matter of time before he would either be doing "hard time" or be dead. Fredie began to wail so loudly that his family could hear him in the apartment above him. When his sister-in-law asked what was wrong, Fredie cried out, "Call Eric!"

When Eric received the call from Fredie's sister-in-law, he immediately enlisted Marco's help. Since they were going into a bad neighborhood, they decided to carry their duty weapons in addition to their Bibles.

A SPIRITUAL BATTLE FOR FREDIE'S SOUL

They arrived at Fredie's home and were escorted into his bedroom, where they found him sitting on the edge of the bed still in tears. Marco knew immediately that there was a spiritual battle going on for Fredie's soul. Pacing frantically around the room, Fredie said he knew he needed a change in his life, but being so deeply involved in his gang, he saw no way out. He believed he had done so much evil that God could not forgive him. At one point, his mother entered the room. She seemed suspicious of Eric and Marco, but after a few minutes, she left the room. The brothers later learned she was a medium and people often came to her in order to contact the dead. Fredie was unable to be still and concentrate on what Eric and Marco were reading to him from their Bibles.

Marco felt an urgency to call on God for help. He told Eric that they needed to stop talking to Fredie and pray. The brothers got down on their knees and began to earnestly plead to God the Father to be merciful to this young man. Imagine this scene: Two police officers on their knees in the bedroom of a hard-core gang banger! It was the love of God being poured into their hearts through the Holy Spirit that brought these two cops to their knees, asking God the Father to rebuke any evil spirits that might be opposing and oppressing

Fredie. They begged God to give this young man a clear mind and open heart to understand and receive the message of salvation through Jesus Christ.

By the time the brothers finished praying, Fredie was calmer and able to listen. That night, Fredie trusted in Jesus Christ as his Lord and Savior. From that moment forward, God began, through the power of His Spirit, to transform Fredie's life. Radical prayer led to radical love and resulted in radical transformation.

Fredie began to attend faithfully the church Marco pastored. The first time he came to Sunday service he was wearing all his gang colors and strutted down the aisle to a front seat. There were many challenging issues that Fredie would have to overcome (not without God's intervention) that concerned Pastor Marco. One issue was "a violation," usually involving a severe beating by gang members to the brink of death as the price for leaving a gang. Pastor Marco began to wonder if they should find a way for Fredie to leave the city.

They looked into several ministries outside of Chicago, but God never opened those doors. As Marco explained, "We meant well, but we sometimes under-estimate what God is able to do. God didn't allow us to get Fredie out of town. He wanted us to continue to show him the love of Jesus. The Holy Spirit was already working in a powerful way, not reforming but transforming him from the inside out without having him leave Chicago."

PROTECTION FOR FREDIE

Pastor Marco, his family, and the church body prayed much for Fredie in the weeks and months following his conversion. One night, when Marco was on police duty, Fredie called his home. Marco's wife, Liz, answered and listened as Fredie explained he was getting ready to face the consequences for leaving his gang. He knew if he did not go to them, they would come looking for him. And if the gang could not find him, they would go after his family.

But Marco later explained how his wife told Fredie he belonged to God and "God was not going to allow the gang to touch a hair on his head."

"I must admit that I didn't have that kind of faith," Marco recalled, "and was sure Fredie would probably get some kind of violation. I just hoped it wouldn't be that severe." Before Fredie ended the call Liz prayed with Fredie. Then he left his home to tell his gang that he was leaving because he now belonged to Jesus Christ.

As Fredie looked for his gang, he discovered that due to conflicts within the gang (including one member stabbing another), the gang broke apart never to unite again. This new believer, with an "immature" confidence in Christ, had sought God the Father's help through prayer and was empowered by the Spirit to take a bold step. To this day, Fredie still lives in Chicago and has never been harmed by either a former or rival gang member.

THE MERCY OF GOD AND THE COURT

A few months after his conversion, Fredie went to speak with Pastor Marco about a legal matter. Prior to his salvation, Fredie had been arrested on gun charges. He explained to Marco that he had hired a lawyer who did work for his gang in the past and that his defense was going to be that the police had planted the guns on him. Two female friends were going to testify to that end on his behalf. However, now that Fredie was Christ's, he was convicted about this false testimony and sought his pastor's advice.

Marco told Fredie what King David did after he had sinned by numbering Israel. God was going to judge David, giving him the choice of one of three consequences. David chose to "fall into the hand of the Lord, for His mercies are great" (2 Sam. 24:11–14, 1 Chron. 21:9–13). Pastor Marco suggested to Fredie that he throw himself at the mercy of God and the mercy of the court. They prayed, and the next day

Fredie called his lawyer and told him he was changing his plea to guilty. The lawyer was stunned and assured Fredie they had a good chance of winning the case with the testimony of the women. But Fredie was determined to do what was right before God, even if it meant going to prison.

Fredie pleaded guilty and asked for mercy. By God's grace, Fredie was told he would receive four months of boot camp, not prison. The church rejoiced with him and continued to pray for him, encouraging him that the sooner he went and finished boot camp, the quicker he would be back serving in the church and growing in the Lord.

The Sunday before Fredie was to turn himself in, the church had a dinner after the service as a time of encouragement before the convicted church member reported back to court. Eric read a testimony he had prepared, sharing all that God had done in Fredie's life in the past six months—how he was growing in his knowledge of the Lord, bringing other gang members to the church, helping to remove a dangerous weapon from the streets, working a full-time job, and securing his own apartment.

Fredie had asked Eric to drive him to the courthouse the day he was to report and, once again, Eric asked Marco to go with him. Eric brought a copy of the testimony he had read at the church dinner, giving it to Fredie and suggesting he give it to the judge. Fredie's lawyer was not enthusiastic about this, thinking it might annoy the judge.

As the judge began to go through the prescribed routine of sentencing Fredie, his lawyer presented him the testimony. The judge did seem annoyed at first, but then began to read it. When done, he asked if the two police officers mentioned in the testimony were present. Upon learning they were, he moved Fredie's case to the end of the day's docket so that he would be able to speak with the two officers.

This was a real surprise to both Marco and Eric. They had not intended, or even imagined, that they would be speaking to the judge on Fredie's behalf. Although the brothers did not think about it at the time, their testifying on behalf of this now ex-gang member would not have been looked upon favorably by the police department or their fellow officers. I told my friend Marco that they had been blinded by the love of Christ to any fears of man and had placed their trust in the Lord (Prov. 29:25).

Marco quickly turned to Eric and said, "What are we going to say?" Eric replied, "You're the preacher, you tell me." So while the judge went through the other cases, the brothers prayed.

The next time Fredie stood before the judge, he had two police officers standing alongside him! They were sworn in and given opportunity to testify to the judge that God had changed Fredie and that they believed he would no longer be in trouble. The state's attorney objected to all this, and so he was allowed by the judge to question the officers. When done, the judge turned to Fredie and asked if he had anything to say before he passed the sentence. Fredie replied, "No, sir."

The judge began by saying that what he was witnessing was unprecedented. (It was unprecedented, of course, because it was being orchestrated by God our Father and not by human beings!) The judge continued by saying that because Marco and Eric were veteran police officers who knew the problems and threats which gang members pose, he was inclined to believe their testimony that Fredie was a changed man. He sentenced Fredie to probation and let him walk out of the courtroom that day.

Fifteen years later, Fredie continues to be a devoted follower of Christ and an elder at the church, serving alongside Pastor Marco and Eric. He is married to a devoted Christian woman he met at the church, has five beautiful children, and works for a major utility company. His life continues to be a blessing to all who know him and serves as a reminder that radical prayer brings forth radical love resulting in radical transformation for the glory of God.

4

RADICAL
PRAYER'S PURPOSE

*Oh Abba—Daddy—please hear my burning
plea! Please keep teaching me, through
Your Spirit, to pray much more effectively
by fueling all of my prayers with Your all-
sufficient and delicious Word, so that each
one of my radical, biblical prayers will be
bold, to hallow Your holy name.
In Jesus' name, Amen!*

IN MY JOURNEY TO become more disciplined in
prayer, I naturally turned to the Bible; and like Jesus'
apostles, I asked my Savior: "Lord, teach *me* to pray."

Not surprisingly, my petition led me directly to
Luke 11:1–13, a portion of Scripture I had read hundreds of times. Only this time, the Spirit graciously
provided me with fresh and unexpected insight that
would further revitalize my personal prayer life.

There are numerous scholarly works available on
this notable portion of Scripture. Therefore, what I
want to share with you here is how this text has come
alive for me by showing me the reason why we pray and
teaching me that God is as sovereign as I am responsible

in how the mystery and power of prayer unfolds.

Luke 11 begins with the lesser-known version of what is typically called "The Lord's Prayer." Luke tells us that Jesus had been praying, and that when He finished, one of His disciples asked Him to teach them to pray.

"TEACH US TO PRAY"

This was a strange request, for Jewish men were very familiar with prayer. They knew from their Scriptures that David and Daniel prayed three times a day (Ps. 55:17; Dan. 6:10). They had read the pleadings of Abraham for the souls in Sodom. They had heard of Moses' intercessions for the stiff-necked people of Israel, and of Isaiah's cries for the Lord not to be furious with His people or remember their iniquity forever (Isa. 64:9). They even had a whole collection of prayers for almost every occasion in the book of Psalms. Moreover, this request itself was made noting that John the Baptist himself had taught his disciples to pray.

But as I reflected anew upon the disciples' request, it struck me that they were not asking Jesus for a "how to" manual on prayer as much as they were asking Him how they could have the same type of intimate relationship with God the Father as He had.

We read Jesus' response in Luke 11:2–4:

So he said to them, "When you pray, say: Our Father in heaven, hallowed be Your name. Your kingdom come. Your will be done on earth as it is in heaven. Give us day by day our daily bread. And forgive us our sins, for we also forgive everyone who is indebted to us. And do not lead us into temptation, but deliver us from the evil one."

Jesus' first instruction was to have the disciples remember who it is they were addressing in prayer—namely, their Father in heaven. Indeed, there is no real prayer without this relationship—a relationship obtained only through the belief that Jesus Christ is God's only begotten Son and the exclusive vehicle through which we address the Father in prayer. And it is only because of this relationship that we can freely and confidently address God as our Father, in Jesus' name, knowing fully that the Holy Spirit will deliver to us the Father's answer to our prayers.

Beloved reader, if you feel your prayer life isn't what it should be, then I plead with you, once again, to immediately take time to examine your faith. As Colin Smith, senior pastor of The Orchard Evangelical Free Church in Illinois, so powerfully put it, "Faith prays." It really is as simple as that.

If you are not praying, then it is time to ask: Where are you placing your faith?

During my time at the cabin, I began to see how I had fallen into the trap of placing my faith in what I was doing for God rather than in who God is and what He was seeking to do in and through me. As a result, my prayer life had been putrid!

In Jeremiah 32:33, God says the people "turned to Me the back, and not the face." Idolatry was at the root of their prayerlessness, as it was at mine. Instead of looking to God—instead of facing Him—the people turned their backs toward Him and, in reality, looked to someone or something else. That is the nature of idolatry.

We cannot have a relationship with someone if we do not spend time facing the person. And when we face someone, we address the individual, we acknowledge who she or he is.

Without faith, there is no basis for prayer and your prayer life will feel empty—as mine did before God woke me up! "Without faith it is impossible to please Him," the Scripture says (Heb. 11:6). But the good news is the verse does not stop there. It goes on to say, "for he who comes to God must believe that He is, and that He is a rewarder of those who diligently seek Him." Here we are given the assurance that God rewards and He hears those who believe in and diligently seek Him.

John 15:7–8 gives another tremendous promise, one in which Jesus Himself declares that the Father would be hallowed. He said, "If you abide in Me, and My words abide in you, you will ask what you desire, and it shall be done for you. By this My Father is glorified, that you bear much fruit; so you will be My disciples."

So in prayer we focus our thoughts on the one we are addressing when we say, "Our Father in heaven." We remind ourselves who it is that we are approaching and why we can have access to Him, through faith in Jesus Christ and through the power of the Holy Spirit (Eph. 2:18). We remind ourselves that this is not just some form of meditation used to calm our inner beings and make us feel better. We are not just talking to the air— we are talking to the God of the universe.

SIX BASIC PETITIONS FOR OUR PRAYERS

Next, Jesus delivers to His disciples six basic petitions for their prayers, beginning with what I now see is our preeminent petition: To hallow God's name.

That the first line of our Lord's prayer— "Hallowed be your name"—was even a petition was something I had never fully grasped. How often had I recited this prayer without really stopping to consider this very first line as a prayer request in and of itself? Until this moment of awareness, I usually thought of these words as "only" an acclamation, an exaltation attached to the opening address.

God used a message by my friend Dr. John Piper, founder and teacher of desiringGod.org, to help me understand that the hallowing of God's name is Jesus' primary prayer request. (His message was presented to a group of pastors in the summer of 2011, not coincidentally the same time as my prayer life was being revolutionized.)

The Son's request to the Father was that the Father's name would be hallowed (or revered). Jesus therefore taught the disciples that the only thing that really mattered in all of life was that God the Father be glorified. That was His ultimate purpose as God's Son, to glorify His Father in all He did.

That should be our primary purpose as well. As the Westminster Catechism so succinctly puts it: "The chief end of man is to glorify God and to enjoy him forever." When we truly understand how worthy God the Father is to be glorified, we will begin to enjoy Him, to spend more time with Him and to be intimate with Him in prayer. This will bring us to true and new levels of joy.

In this very first petition, then, Jesus gave His disciples the reason *why* we must pray—for the hallowing of the Father's name. He gave them a deeper look into the intimate relationship He had with the Father and revealed His motivation for prayer, which I believe is really what the disciples were looking for when they asked their question in the first place.

Dr. Piper further helped me understand the significance of our "hallowing" by noting that it is the only one of the six petitions that involves a response of the human heart. In his 2011 message referenced earlier, Piper said:

> In this petition, we hear explicitly (it may be implicit in the others, but only here is it explicit)—we hear the one specific response of the human heart that God requires of all human beings—the hallowing, reverencing, honoring, esteeming, admiring, valuing, treasuring of God's name above all things. None of the other five requests tells us explicitly to pray for a specific human response of the heart.[1]

After teaching the disciples that the *why* of prayer is the hallowing of the Father's name, which involves a response of the heart, Jesus then instructs them on the *what* of prayer. Again, with the help of Dr. Piper's teaching, I saw that the remaining five petitions in Luke 11:2–4 all support the first, supreme petition that God's name be hallowed:

1. God's name will be hallowed when His kingdom comes; that is, when His kingdom will one day be established in the new heavens and new earth. So we must pray for the return of Christ and the establishment of His kingdom.

2. God's name will be hallowed when His will is done on earth; that is, when His followers live in obedience to His commands. We must, therefore, pray as the French Protestant Reformer John Calvin did, that God's invisible kingdom would become visible through His people in all their conduct.

3. God's name will be hallowed when He provides daily bread. He is glorified when He provides for His children's basic needs. So we must pray for God to supply those needs.

4. God's name will be hallowed when He forgives our sin and especially when we, in turn, forgive others; that is, God is glorified when we can forgive someone else, remembering the great mercy that God first showed us. So we must pray for the ability to forgive others when we have been wronged.

5. God's name will be hallowed when He gives us victory over temptation; that is, God is glorified when He keeps us from doing evil. So we must pray for the ability to withstand temptation and the ability to choose whatever is true, honorable, just, pure, lovely, commendable, and excellent (see Phil. 4:8).

When I began to fully grasp that our aim, at all times, is to hallow God's holy name, my prayer life was transformed. Take the petition for daily bread, for example. Previously, I would ask God to supply my family's needs, which Jesus tells us is something we should pray for. However, I now realized that I needed to make this request more out of my concern for God's glory than for my family's actual needs. In other words, I now ask God the Father to provide my daily bread so that I will have energy to hallow His name through prayer. I ask for my family's provisions so that they, too, will be able to hallow God's name and live lives that show others the faithfulness of God.

I saw that praying for God to keep me from temptation and to deliver me from the evil one was not so much about my avoiding the painful consequences of sin as it was that God's name would be glorified through the testimony of my transformed life. How can I come into His presence to hallow His name in prayer if I am involved in sin? How can I testify to others of His transforming power if I give in to the sinful temptations around me? I can't. Therefore, I pray that God will deliver me from temptation and keep me from sinning in order that I may glorify Him in all that I do.

A PARABLE ON GLORIFYING GOD

That the hallowing of God the Father's name is our first priority was also emphasized by Jesus in the parable He told immediately after giving His disciples this pattern for prayer.

Jesus told parables, which were very human and therefore very relatable stories, to teach us spiritual truths. It is often said that parables are earthly stories with heavenly meaning. So for many of the parables, we need to ask two questions: Which character represents me? And which character represents God? This will help us understand the point of Jesus' story.

Here is the parable Jesus told, as recorded in Luke 11:5–8.

> And He said to them, "Which of you shall have a friend, and go to him at midnight and say to him, 'Friend, lend me three loaves; for a friend of mine has come to me on his journey, and I have nothing to set before him'; and he will answer from within and say, 'Do not trouble me; the door is now shut, and my children are with me in bed; I cannot rise and give to you'? I say to you, though he will not rise and give to him because he is his friend, yet because of his persistence he will rise and give him as many as he needs."

In this case, it is easy to figure out which character represents you and me, because Jesus tells us right at the start. He asked the disciples to pretend they have approached a friend, at midnight, to ask for food for another friend who has made a journey to see them. While it is easy to see the character who represents us, it is humbling to actually make the identification. To do this, we need to admit we are the person who is unprepared, the one who has nothing to offer another friend in need.

Take a moment to let what I just wrote really sink in. Before this man could help someone else, he needed to confess his own need of help. This was not a simple request for a few loaves of bread. In the Middle Eastern culture of Jesus' time, hospitality was (and still is) a very important priority. It would be embarrassing for the one unprepared, and a great insult to the one who is the guest, if a proper welcome was not given. The unexpected visit from a friend exposed the need within the host's own house, "I have nothing to set before him." Jesus is asking us to admit that we are like beggars.

So let's stop pretending and take a radical timeout. Let's come clean and become real with God our Father, by approaching Him through radical, biblical prayer in Jesus' name. Let's turn our faces, not our backs, to God our Father. Let's get down on our knees, become shameless beggars, and tell God that we want Him alone to be the only object of our affection in order that we may hallow His supreme, majestic, holy name. And let us be diligent in praying that the very name of God Himself would be valued and treasured by all peoples everywhere.

5

RADICAL PRAYER'S PERSISTENCE

*My loving heavenly Father, cleanse me with hyssop and create within my heart a deeper capacity to receive and retain Your irresistible and transformative love. Empower my heart with fresh passion to love You and hence love and embrace anyone You send my way, regardless of what he or she has done or where he or she has come from.
In Jesus' name, Amen!*

IN THE PREVIOUS CHAPTER I said that in many of the parables of Jesus, we have to ask ourselves two questions.

The first question is, Who in the parable represents "me"? For example, in chapter 4 we recognized that in Jesus' parable in Luke 11, you and I are the person found wanting; pounding at the door, urgently seeking help. The beggar.

In this chapter, we'll look at the second question we must ask ourselves, namely: Which character in the story represents God? And the answer may surprise you!

Let's read the parable from Luke 11:5–8 again:

And He said to them, "Which of you shall
have a friend, and go to him at midnight and
say to him, 'Friend, lend me three loaves; for
a friend of mine has come to me on his journey, and I have nothing to set before him'; and
he will answer from within and say, 'Do not
trouble me; the door is now shut, and my children are with me in bed; I cannot rise and give
to you'? I say to you, though he will not rise
and give to him because he is his friend, yet
because of his persistence he will rise and give
him as many as he needs."

As strange as it might seem, the character who
represents God here is the friend already in bed. That's
right, the man behind the closed door. The one responding to "our" repeated pounding on the door with:
"Don't bother me, I can't help you right now."

Not exactly the way we envision our prayer-
answering God!

And yet, if we're honest, we all have at one time or
another thought of God in just this way. Slow to respond. Unwilling to help. Much like Mary and Martha
found Jesus when He delayed going to heal their brother

Lazarus when he was sick and dying (John 11:1–15, 20–22).

But now see how this story of "shameless persistence" plays out.

PARABLE ON FAITHFULNESS

Both men find themselves in the culture of the Middle East, where hospitality is exceedingly important. It would be embarrassing for the one unprepared, and a great insult to the guest, if a proper welcome was not given. And even though this was an unexpected visit at a very unusual hour (midnight), the culture demanded that something be provided. So, in order to save face, the man seeks help, driven to the point of making a nuisance of himself in order to feed his friend.

But no less influenced by this cultural understanding is the man in bed. Would not this same emphasis on hospitality also demand that the man behind the closed door arise to share with *his* neighbor in need?

On this critical point, Pastor Tom Stuart argues in his blog that "a major theme of this entire passage on prayer is about the nature of the Father and His response to prayer." Stuart writes,

A person's name and reputation were at stake when called upon to open one's home and share one's possessions with a person in need. If word got out that a man had denied his neighbor help in time of need it would be a shame to him and his name. Any self-respecting householder would choose "no-shame" in answer to pleas for bread. This is the case for the man in his bed, and even more importantly our Father who is in heaven.

So this is the insight that we have missed in truly understanding this parable. We thought it was a challenge to be shameless in our persistence in prayer. But it is much more about our heavenly Father being true to His name and nature. We thought it was all about our faith when really it is all about God's faithfulness.[1]

This view aligns beautifully with what the disciples were seeking earlier regarding the intimacy Jesus had with the Father. Therefore, to encourage the disciples in their praying, it would make great sense for Jesus to instruct them about the one to whom they were praying.

The wonderful thing here is that the would-be host in Jesus' story knew the right person to go to in his time of need. His friend, who had come a long distance, may not have known the person behind the door, but the "beggar" did. He knew he had found the right person to supply his need, to prevent him from being shamed. And he was now providing the one in bed with an opportunity to bring glory to himself by supplying this request.

We say we know God has all that we need for life. The question is: Do we really believe that? Are we fully convinced that He has exactly what we need? Are we totally committed to looking to God alone? If we say that God is the only one who can supply all our needs, then why do we so often look to others to do so? Instead, our attitude toward prayer should be: I am not going anywhere until God my Father opens the door and gives me what I need to bless my neighbor, for the hallowing of His holy name!

PERSISTING IN OUR PRAYERS

By emphasizing His Father's faithfulness, Jesus motivated His disciples—and motivates us today!—to persist in our prayers.

I have seen and experienced indisputable evidence that God our loving Father delights in answering our radical, biblical prayers when our "persistence" is driven by our knowing that He is faithful. That He is able.

And we can only know of God's faithfulness if we have an intimate relationship with Him!

It is the context of this intimate relationship with the God who is faithful that Jesus says we can persistently ask, seek, and knock on the one door for the Father's answer:

> "So I say to you, ask, and it will be given to you; seek, and you will find; knock, and it will be opened to you. For everyone who asks receives, and he who seeks finds, and to him who knocks it will be opened. If a son asks for bread from any father among you, will he give him a stone? Or if he asks for a fish, will he give him a serpent instead of a fish? Or if he asks for an egg, will he offer him a scorpion? If you then, being evil, know how to give good gifts to your children, how much more will your heavenly Father give the Holy Spirit to those who ask Him!" (Luke 11: 9–13)

After declaring, "So I say to you," Jesus gave the disciples three commands, each followed by a promise. He told the disciples to ask, seek, and knock, and then promised if they did they would receive, they would find, and the door would be opened.

In the original language, each of these verbs is an imperative in the present tense, denoting an emphatic command. The Greek word for "ask" is *aiteite*, which means to beg or petition. The word for "seek" is *zeteite*, which means to search for or desire. *Krouete* is the word translated as "knock" and literally means to strike against something and was the common word for "knock" in the Greek language. These are action words—action words that carry with them the idea of heightened immediacy!

Does it seem difficult for you to pray? Seize this HUGE promise. Ask, seek, and knock! God will see to it that you receive and find—and that closed doors will be opened to you!

Two words of caution should be given here, however. The first is against thinking that we can badger, pester, or harangue God into answering our prayers if we just "keep at it." A danger here, and it can begin subtly, is that we move our faith from God Himself and place it on our efforts—the amount of or the intensity of our praying.

The second caution may seem counterintuitive: Our persistence may actually paralyze us. In the Midwestern culture in which I primarily minister, this kind of persistence is thought of as almost rude and inappropriate. Therefore, we may be prone to quickly dismiss this parable because of our discomfort over such persistence and not take time to wrestle with the possibility that Jesus is teaching us something that should shake up how we usually pray!

Both of these tendencies can be tempered by remembering one other thing about prayer that is also taught in Luke 11:1–13: When we honor God's name, we have the duty to be persistent, and we can come confidently before our loving heavenly Father when we do so on behalf of others.

It is in light of who God is and our persistence to hallow His name that Jesus gives the disciples the assurance that their heavenly Father will give good answers to their prayers. If human, earthly fathers know how to give good responses to their children's requests, how much more can the heavenly Father do! The contrast is so severe that Jesus even uses the word "evil" to describe the best earthly father when compared to the heavenly Father. Jesus was telling His disciples that God would never shortchange them. He would never exchange evil for good. And they could count on that answer because He, Jesus, had firsthand and personal knowledge of the Father.

Our persistence, then, becomes fully motivated and driven by our loving obedience to God our Father and our passionate desire to hallow His holy name.

Thus, as we ask, seek, and knock at the one door, we can be ever confident that our Father will answer.

PUTTING PERSISTENCE INTO PRACTICE

I met Diego in Louisiana on Easter weekend of 2002. A native of Colombia, South America, he connected with me immediately; soon we would become committed friends. There in the deep South, in the land of crawfish and Cajun spices, this Cuban was surprised to find someone who spoke the language of heaven (Spanish, that is) and appreciated a good dish of rice and black beans.

I was with a large group accompanying Chuck Colson, founder of Prison Fellowship, on his traditional Easter services in prison. We were at the Louisiana State Penitentiary, better known as Angola, named after the small post office that serves the prison. Yes, Diego was an inmate at Angola.

Five years earlier, Diego had been found guilty of possession with intent to distribute heroin. He received a harsh and unprecedented sentence for his first-time drug offense—life imprisonment—and was sent to Angola, once the bloodiest prison in the United States. However, under the innovative leadership of Warden Burl Cain, this once bloody prison has now become one of the least violent prisons. And for Diego, Angola became the place where he was confronted by the truth of Jesus Christ and invaded by the grace of God.

I often tell inmates it is better to make it to heaven in prison than to hell on the street. Diego repented of his sins, confessed with his mouth, and believed in his heart that God the Father had raised Jesus from the dead (Rom. 10:9–10). His relationship with our triune God brought him a new purpose in life.

Diego earned an accredited bachelor of arts degree in Christian ministry from the New Orleans Baptist Theological Seminary while in prison and became an inmate minister. He spoke to groups of teenagers who toured the prison as part of their Confirmation classes and spent time developing his gift of painting. But his real passion was his work with the prison's hospice program, so he became a certified hospice worker.

When assigned a patient, he would be on call 24/7 to lovingly and tirelessly attend to that individual's physical and spiritual needs. (Allowing inmate ministers to move about the prison is one of Warden Cain's innovations that has brought about a positive change in the prison's culture.) Diego often told me that he had no problem with changing a man's diaper because he could do it with the love of Christ and through the power of the Holy Spirit. Forty-seven inmates breathed their last breath with Diego by their side.

Over the years, Diego had unsuccessfully gone through a series of appeals in an attempt to overturn his conviction or reduce his sentence. This was very costly financially and emotionally for him and his family. Amazingly, he was eventually granted a hearing before the Louisiana Parole and Pardon Board, and asked Tom and Wendy Horton and me to attend the hearing and speak on his behalf. The entire prison population, inmates as well as officials, were interested in the outcome. Since Diego had received a life sentence as a first-time offender and for a drug-related case, this hearing was important. A precedent could possibly be set.

I was scheduled to preach in the chapel service at the main prison compound the same evening as Diego's hearing. We anticipated the service would be a time of celebration. But the hearing did not go well. Diego was denied parole. The enthusiasm and hope that had permeated the prison over the days leading up to the hearing dissipated like air from a deflated balloon. When it was time for the evening service, I was not sure if Diego would attend. But there he was, as was his custom, greeting me with a bottle of cold water and a towel to wipe my sweat. He was testifying to the power of Christ within him by the gracious way he was responding to this adversity.

RADICAL, BIBLICAL PRAYER FOR DIEGO

Of course, we began to pray. This was an opportunity for me to put into practice what I had learned from Luke 11; that is, that our prayers should concern the needs of others, not just ourselves; that we need to persist in praying; and, above all, our praying should be for the hallowing of God's name. Therefore, my prayers now were not just *for* Diego. Rather, I was more concerned for the hallowing of God's name *through* Diego himself and his situation.

Usually when someone is denied parole, they have to wait three years before reapplying for another hearing. But prompted by the Holy Spirit, I began to pray that Diego would be given a second hearing within six months! This was a bold request. The Hortons and others joined me in this radical, biblical prayer. This would be something only God could do. Only He could move the hearts of the officials to grant another hearing so quickly and be open to Diego returning to his family in Colombia. Even the ungodly would have to acknowledge that no human being could orchestrate this.

We prayed to the God who is like no other, the one who acts on behalf of those who wait for Him (Isa. 64:4). Within six months, the Hortons and I returned to Angola for Diego's second hearing. This time the outcome was favorable. God moved!

Soon after the hearing, the extradition process started. Diego was sent to a parish jail to await traveling to Colombia. At the jail he was able to testify about Jesus Christ to over forty-five Hispanics and dozens of English-speaking men. God's name was hallowed!

When he arrived in Colombia, he was reunited with his large family. However, it was bittersweet, for his mother had passed away two years earlier. God was gracious, though, in allowing Diego to have some time with his dad before his father died. I know it was important for Diego, who had cared for so many at Angola, to be able to attend to his very own father in his last days.

Things were not easy for Diego in Colombia. He had difficulty finding work and finding an evangelical church body with whom he could worship and fellowship. The Hortons and I kept in touch with him through phone calls and emails; we even began praying about traveling to see him. In April of 2014, we heard from Diego's daughter that he had suffered a fatal heart attack. We were comforted by knowing that Diego was buried next to his parents in his homeland of Colombia and not in the inmate cemetery at Angola.

But most importantly, we rejoiced that Diego was now present with his gracious heavenly Father.

THE POWER OF BOLD, PERSISTENT PRAYER

Dear reader, reflect on Diego's story—and the power of bold, persistent prayer.

Would you take a radical time-out and repent of whatever wrong perceptions you have of the God who is faithful to answer the prayers of His people? Ask the Father to give you a deeper understanding of who He is. Spend time reading and praying Scriptures that tell of His wonderful power and glory. If you do so, you will have a renewed and fresh confidence for radical, biblical prayer. And you will know beyond a shadow of doubt that He is a good, loving, and faithful heavenly Father who always has your best interests at heart. Why? Because through you and me His desire is His glory and your hallowing of His holy name.

6

RADICAL PRAYER'S POWER

*My Father and my God, I am coming to You
with confidence and boldness, yet with fresh
humility, asking You to fill me afresh in
Your Spirit and to grant me through Your
Holy Spirit the very heart of Jesus Christ so I
might walk in His resurrection power. In
that way may I become one with You as
Jesus is one with You. ¡Aleluya!
In Jesus' name, Amen!*

THERE IS ONE LAST PART OF Jesus' teaching from
Luke 11 that captured my attention: "If you then,
being evil, know how to give good gifts to your children, how much more will your heavenly Father give
the Holy Spirit to those who ask Him!" (v. 13).

There He was—the Holy Spirit. Third person
of the Trinity. Jesus Christ, the second person of the
Trinity, was telling the disciples that God the Father
would not just hear their prayers but would answer
their prayers—and that answer was *God Himself* in the
person of the Holy Spirit.

Many years ago, I had a conversation with a well-known "charismatic" pastor. He challenged me by saying, "You evangelicals have a different Trinity than we do." Puzzled, I asked him to clarify. He responded, "Your Trinity is God the Father, God the Son, and the Bible."

It took me a few seconds to process, but then I understood what he was saying. Many of us have elevated God's Word—as essential as it is—above God the Holy Spirit; and this, in spite of what that same book tells us about this third person of the Trinity.

THE HOLY SPIRIT:
OUR CHALLENGER AND LIFE CHANGER

My dear reader, I urge you to take a radical time-out right now. Pray for God's name to be hallowed in you by giving you a greater understanding of the Holy Spirit. Let His perfect love cast out any fears or confusions you may have regarding this Comforter, Challenger, and Changer. Trust what the Father and Son have said: That the Holy Spirit is a good gift and that He comes to you loaded with good treasures for your benefit. Take time to read these Scriptures and learn that:

+ The Holy Spirit is our Helper and Teacher (John 14:16, 26).

- The Holy Spirit reveals more about Christ (John 15:26–27).
- The Holy Spirit gives the confidence we need in order to call God "Abba! Father!" (Gal. 4:6).
- The Holy Spirit brings hope by giving us wisdom and understanding of all that the gospel means (Eph. 1:17–18).
- The Holy Spirit regenerates us (John 3:5–8).
- The Holy Spirit transforms us (Gal. 5:22–23).
- The Holy Spirit equips us for service (1 Cor. 12:4–11).

But we cannot forget that the Holy Spirit can also be quenched. Immediately following his exhortation to the Thessalonians to pray without ceasing, the apostle Paul warns them not to quench the Spirit (1 Thess. 5:19). In the seven other New Testament uses of the Greek word translated "quench," all are speaking about the putting out of fire. It is for sure that if we have been truly saved by faith and regenerated by the Holy Spirit, He will never depart from us. As I like to tell the men and women in prison, the Holy Spirit came to *own* your house, not *rent* it! However, it is possible for us to so suppress Him, to so ignore Him as to render Him powerless in our lives. Isn't it interesting that this warning comes immediately after the exhortation to pray without ceasing?

During my days at the cabin, I realized what had happened to me. I had quenched the Holy Spirit. In my zeal to proclaim, in this age of relativism, that there indeed was such a thing as absolute truth and that we could find it in the Word of God, I had lost sight of the Holy Spirit. I had slipped into the trap of relying on my power to energize me and my ministry, rather than the power of the Holy Spirit.

As soon as I repented of this, the Holy Spirit filled me afresh with His glorious anointing and renewed my hope in Christ. In addition to understanding that my prayers needed to be fueled by the Word of God, I now realized that my prayers needed to be oiled by the Holy Spirit. Indeed, as oil lubricates the individual parts of an engine so it can function properly, so too the Holy Spirit keeps all of the parts of my life in Christ—my prayers, my activities, my very being—running effectively on all cylinders so that all I do and say can hallow the name of the Father.

The "mysteriousness" of the Holy Spirit is what makes many North American believers uncomfortable. We like to quantify, define, make our bullet lists, and draw pictures to explain things. We cannot do that with the Holy Spirit.

In his *Lectures to My Students*, Spurgeon taught of the necessity of the anointing of the Holy Spirit. He wrote,

> Everyone knows what the freshness of the morning is when orient pearls abound on every blade of grass, but who can describe it, much less produce it of itself? Such is the mystery of spiritual anointing. We know, but we cannot tell to others what it is. It is as easy as it is foolish, to counterfeit it. Unction is a thing which you cannot manufacture, and its counterfeits are worse than worthless. Yet it is, in itself, priceless, and beyond measure needful if you would edify believers and bring sinners to Christ.[1]

Spiritual anointing—or unction—is not just for those who are in "full-time Christian ministry." *Every* believer has been given the Holy Spirit (Eph. 1:13). Jesus promised the disciples that the heavenly Father would give the Holy Spirit as a good gift in response to their prayers (Luke 11:13). Moreover, you have all of the Holy Spirit you will ever need because God the Father gives the Holy Spirit without measure (John 3:34)! So, once again, dear reader, I urge you to pray for the hallowing of God's name by praying not for more of the Holy Spirit but for the Holy Spirit to have more of you.

"The truth is," wrote E. M. Bounds, "if we cannot pray for the Holy Spirit we cannot pray for any good thing from God, for He is the sum of all good to us."[2] Bounds continues, "How complex, confusing and involved is many a human direction about obtaining the gift of the Holy Spirit as the abiding Comforter, our Sanctifier, and the one who empower us! How simple and direct is our Lord's direction—ASK!"[3]

FROM THE GATE TO INSIDE THE PRISON

Seven months after my time at the cabin, the Hortons and I ministered together for three days at the Inner Change Freedom Initiative (Prison Fellowship's re-entry program) in the Minnesota Correctional Center at Lino Lakes. Our time concluded with a powerful communion service during which we saw many men repent and relationships begin healing. Tom Horton had been challenging me to do more of this kind of in-prison ministry, and this experience awakened in me a deep desire to see the same thing happen in Illinois.

For twenty-one years, our ministry had been focused on meeting Christian inmates at the prison gate upon their release and facilitating their transition back into society. Introducing a new direction in our ministry could be risky. But I remembered what the Holy Spirit had said to me during my cabin experience—that I would live to see a revival in the church in America and that it would come from the prisons.

I remembered hearing the story of Bill Bright, founder of Campus Crusade for Christ (now known as Cru), spreading a map of the world on his kitchen table and crying out to the Lord to give him the world. Barbara and I located a listing of the Illinois Department of Corrections (IDOC) adult correctional centers and began praying that if we were to spend more time within the prisons, God would surprise us by opening doors of opportunity which clearly came without our "manipulating" them.

He did! Shortly after our time in Minnesota, I received a surprising telephone call from the chief chaplain of IDOC, Stephen Keim. He was fairly new on the job, filling a position that had been vacant for several years. His IDOC supervisor suggested he meet with me, so he was calling to introduce himself and offered to drive to Wheaton for a meeting.

"CAN YOU HELP FEED MY SHEEP?"

Within a few days, we were meeting for lunch at the same restaurant where I got the phone call about Barbara's crash. We were exchanging the usual pleasantries when suddenly Chief Keim leaned over his lunch and abruptly asked: "Manny, the fifty-thousand-plus inmates in the IDOC are starving for truth! Can you help feed my sheep?"

Stunned, I answered, "Yes." Then I told the chief: "I don't know the *how*, but I do know the WHO who knows the how!"

I had no idea how our little ministry could help with this request, but I was confident my heavenly Father knew! To underscore that point, I told Chief Keim that God had recently brought to fruition a desire of mine to offer theological education to IDOC inmates at Danville Correctional Center by using a devoted group of Christian brothers from northwest Indiana (led by a pig farmer and a garbage man!) to establish the Divine Hope Reformed Bible Seminary there. If our God could do the "impossible" once, I told the chief, He could most certainly do it again! To bring the truth of the Gospel to over fifty thousand men and women was a request worthy of shameless asking, seeking, and knocking; and I was confident that God would answer by giving, finding, and opening.

Chief Keim also told me about a gardening program that was starting at one of the prisons. He was working on obtaining seeds and agricultural tools and decided to write to a few churches listed in the Yellow

Pages to seek funding for this pilot project. He asked me if I had ever heard of Willow Creek Church, one of those he had randomly picked from the telephone book. I laughed and then explained that my dear friend Tom Horton had been a part of the original group that started the church.

I reached for my cellphone to call Tom, but not before telling Chief Keim the story of how Tom and I met.

In 2006, Tom's wife, Wendy, had attended her mother's church one Sunday and heard an appeal for volunteers for a special event called Returning Hearts. This event was organized by Awana Lifeline and was designed to allow children to visit their fathers who were incarcerated at Angola. (I am humbled that God allowed me, even during my years of lean prayers, to introduce Awana to Angola and challenge them to consider ministry to children of inmates. Pure grace!)

Wendy and her sister signed up to act as family chaperones, but then Wendy's sister had to change her plans. Tom did not like the idea of his wife going to a men's maximum security prison by herself. But seeing that Wendy was firm on going, Tom decided the only thing he could do was join her.

In God's sovereignty, the Hortons and I were on the same flight from Chicago to Baton Rouge, and at the baggage claim we figured out we were heading to the same place.

That weekend the Holy Spirit did a work in both their hearts and cultivated in them a desire to be involved in prison ministry, as they saw the inmates as people who matter to God, the heavenly Father. Although they had both been Christians for some time, they were not involved in any ministries together nor were they involved in any work that stretched them spiritually. It was the start of a new chapter in their marriage as well as our friendship.

I made the call to Tom, introduced him to Chief Keim over the phone, and asked for his help in seeing if Willow Creek could provide the seeds and tools needed for the gardening project. Over the coming years, the Holy Spirit was gracious to take this introduction and simple request and do with it "exceedingly abundantly above all that we ask or think" (Eph. 3:20). Not only did Willow Creek supply all that was needed for that project, they increased their involvement in various jail and prison ministries. In 2013, for example, Willow Creek partnered with the IDOC to distribute Christmas packages containing Gospel materials and treats to over twenty thousand inmates and correctional officers. This required tackling all the typical logistical challenges of such a project as well as all the additional safety and security issues that are part of prison life. In 2014, over thirty-two thousand packages were delivered. And at the time of this writing, Willow Creek has set a goal of distributing Christmas packages to every one of Chief Keim's 50,000-plus "sheep"!

When I returned home after my lunch with Chief Keim, I began to cry out to the Lord about the chaplain's request. In response, the Holy Spirit brought to my remembrance the few extended seminars we had done in prisons earlier in our ministry. Knowing that two or three days of teaching could have greater effect on Illinois' inmate population than quick in-and-out sermons, Barbara and I sketched out what a weekend ministry "assault" might look like: Times for singing and teaching God's Word, question and answer sessions, stories, and testimonies.

Our youngest son was still in high school at this time, so Barbara was not free to commit to the travel such a ministry redirection would require. However, since the Hortons had already accompanied me on several multi-day prison visits, they seemed the perfect partners to join in this new adventure. And they agreed! Even though it meant taking their personal vacation time to do so, they responded with great excitement.

We presented our big idea of a weekend ministry to Chief Keim and received his approval to give it a try. In December of 2011 the Hortons and I headed to Robinson Correctional Center for the first of what would come to be called "Freedom God's Way" weekends. We found what Chief Keim said to be true—the inmates were hungry to hear truth. Since then, we have been able to proclaim the Gospel and strengthen inmate believers at least once in twenty-six of the twenty-seven adult correctional centers in the IDOC. Since 2012, the Hortons and I have spent on average twelve weekends each year ministering to the men and women in the IDOC through Freedom God's Way.

TIME TO PRAY AND OBEY
AT STATEVILLE CORRECTIONAL CENTER

My prayers that God's name would be hallowed throughout the Illinois Department of Corrections intensified. Again, it was not for me to devise the ways in which that would be done. God Himself would have to show me the how. God Himself would have to choose those whom He would redeem, revive, and restore. My responsibility was to pray and then obey when He opened the door. He opened that door when the Hortons and I arrived at Stateville Correctional Center, one of Illinois' most notorious maximum security prisons, for a special one-day Freedom God's Way.

Expecting to be escorted to the gym, where we

usually met, we were asked to move to the theater. Typically, unarmed correctional officers remained with us in the room. But this time, we saw detectives with pistols around us and then realized there were two officers stationed in towers above us overlooking the room, each bearing an automatic rifle. It was like a scene from the movies. When we inquired about these changes and the presence of all the "guns," we were told that the room contained many rival gang members. Completely unknown to us, the chaplain arranged for the top one hundred gang chiefs and leaders to be in attendance!

Most of the men sat with tattooed arms crossed over their chests as if challenging us to tell them something they didn't already know. Many had teardrops tattooed under their eyes, each drop representing someone they had killed. These were the inmates who caused trouble and unrest within the prison.

Before we even got started, a gang leader named Freddy disrespected Wendy with both his looks and his language. Imagine the restraint Tom needed to exercise! We each cried out silently to God our Father to make us both wise and bold in our responses. He lovingly answered us by giving the Holy Spirit in extra measure, empowering Wendy and Tom to do their parts in storytelling and testimonies, and anointing me to preach the gospel of Jesus Christ.

At the end of the day, over eighty men—including Freddy—stood to publicly profess their faith in Christ as Savior and Lord. They repented from their sins and "dropped their flags," meaning they publicly declared their resignation from their gangs. This was a bold step. Dropping a flag could cost them their lives. Freddy even apologized to Wendy for being disrespectful. We rejoiced greatly in God being gracious to these men and drawing them to Himself.

JUST JAILHOUSE CONVERSIONS?

When we returned home and shared what God had done, many rejoiced with us. However, we could tell some were skeptical, probably thinking these were just "jailhouse conversions." God would give us assurance that for one man, Freddy, his belief was the real deal.

About eighteen months after our day at Stateville, Freddy was transferred from prison to the Lake County Jail so he could attend a hearing concerning a reduction in his sentence. This in itself was highly unusual. What was also unusual was that Wendy, once a typical suburban homemaker and personal trainer, had become a volunteer chaplain at the Lake County Jail in addition to spending one weekend a month with her husband and me in prison.

Freddy recognized Wendy during one of her visits

and called out, "Christmas socks!" (This was the name he had mockingly given her in Stateville but now used fondly.) Freddy then told her he had just come from Bible study and had been walking with the Lord Jesus since that redemptive day at Stateville.

A few days later, Tom and I had the privilege of joining Wendy for a "mini" one-day Freedom God's Way at the jail and were delighted to be able to worship and fellowship with Freddy, the former gang chief who is now our brother in Christ.

Freddy continues to grow his faith through studying God's Word and testifying to his former gang members of the redemption that is available through the work of Jesus Christ on the cross. By the mercy of God, Freddy's sentence was reduced by twenty years. His behavior improved so much so that he was transferred from Stateville to a lower security level prison. Soon he will leave prison—a very different man than the one who entered.

Because of our increased involvement within the prisons, God opened the door for the Hortons to take several of the IDOC officials to Angola to meet with Warden Cain and to see the transformation that had taken place in that once bloody prison. God had also placed on Tom's heart the desire to do a Freedom God's Way at the Pontiac (Illinois) Correctional Center.

AN "IMPOSSIBLE AND BOLD PRAYER REQUEST"

Pontiac houses over 2,200 men. Of those, about 1,800 are in some kind of segregation unit. This means they are confined or restricted more than a typical inmate. These men have brought this upon themselves by not behaving well when in the general prison population. Most were transferred to Pontiac from other prisons within the IDOC as a last measure of punishment for either severe misbehavior or even new crimes committed while incarcerated, such as an assault on another inmate or officer. They are confined to their cells for twenty-four hours a day, seven days a week, except for a weekly shower and trips to the exercise cage twice a week. They have no other privileges. While some may have limited non-contact visits, others have no contact with people except prison officials.

Requesting to hold a Freedom God's Way weekend at Pontiac certainly fit my definition of what I was now calling an "impossible *and bold* prayer request." Not only were we asking to meet with those who were not supposed to get privileges such as this, but we knew that what we were asking would present challenges for the warden and his security staff.

Tom made his appeal to the warden and his staff via conference call to allow us to do a Freedom God's Way weekend at Pontiac. The warden hesitated and asked Tom, "Do you understand that who we have here are the worst of the worst?" Outwardly, Tom replied, "Yes, sir," but then added to himself, *Good! That way when they get "corrected" we'll know who really did it!* We knew that if Jesus could transform a Saul of Tarsus into the apostle Paul, He could transform anyone. So we began to pray, and God began to move.

The warden reluctantly agreed to allow us to meet with eight men and then graciously granted us the whole weekend!

FREEDOM GOD'S WAY

We were not sure what to expect when the time came for us to go to Pontiac. However, we went confidently in the power of the Holy Spirit, trusting Him to do all that Scripture promised He would. The men shuffled in, one by one, each escorted by an officer who maintained control through holding a chain attached to the prisoner's waist, like you would a dog on a leash. Their ankles were shackled together with chains that attached to their waists, limiting leg movement. Their hands were also chained to their waists, severely limiting their ability to hold a Bible or turn a page. Once they were seated on the narrow metal bench protruding from a cold cinderblock wall, they were shackled by the waist into hooks in the wall.

Once again we entrusted ourselves to our heavenly Father, asking Him to glorify Himself by bringing these men to faith in Christ. Never before had we had such an opportunity to proclaim Freedom God's Way to men who were both spiritually and physically captive!

The men were genuinely attentive and engaged throughout the morning. We wondered, though, if they would all return after lunch. Would they want to spend a couple more hours sitting in such a restricted manner? To our delight, all eight returned for the afternoon, then again all day Saturday, and again on Sunday morning. By the end of the weekend, each man had made a profession of faith in Christ. The Hortons and I were humbled to share the Lord's Supper with them (something we had only recently added to the weekend). And we were moved watching these new brothers bend their heads and maneuver the Communion elements joyfully into their mouths.

As of this writing, we have returned to do two more weekends at Pontiac, each time at the *warden's request*! During the three weekends, we ministered to twenty-five men. In addition, the warden has granted permission for a team of volunteers, led by the Hortons, to do cell-by-cell visitation in the segregation units once a month. Lastly, we've learned that each of the eight men who attended the very first weekend have been allowed to return to their original prisons because of their improved behavior. Although still captive physically, these men are now living free in Christ.

These events illustrate what the anointing of the Spirit looks like in the life of the believer. It is what I call 100 percent God's sovereignty and 100 percent man's responsibility. As the great preacher Charles Spurgeon said, it is not easy to define and hard to describe, but you know it when you see it. In God's absolute sovereignty, He arranged for me to meet the Hortons. In God's absolute sovereignty, He moved Chief Keim to call me. But I was responsible to hallow God's holy name. I was responsible to be obedient to His command to pray (see Luke 18:1–14).

It is like a divine dance. When men pray in the power of the Holy Spirit, God moves.

7

RADICAL PRAYER'S LOVE

Father, You are the God of the impossible! You can do anything. Surprise me, my Father. I pray to You with radical and relentless passion that You will grant me the courage and zeal of Moses to defend Your glory. Pour over me his same abundant faith to intercede in prayer for my neighbors' redemption. Grant me the perseverance of Moses to never give up, and the capacity of Moses to suffer with joy for the hallowing of Your holy name.
In Jesus' name, Amen!

AS GOD THE FATHER gives more of the Holy Spirit in response to our passionate, persistent praying, we will have an increased love for Him and for our neighbor. And who is my neighbor? Anyone who God sovereignly sends my way!

This increased love results in a greater joy and desire to serve both God and man. We validate our love for God the Father by loving our neighbor, regardless of who that neighbor is, where she comes from, or what he has done. As the apostle Paul put it, we are debtors of grace "both to Greeks and to barbarians, both to wise and to unwise" (Rom. 1:14).

One of my favorite Bible characters is Moses. His whole life is a picture of the good tension between God's absolute sovereignty and human responsibility —a tension that plays out repeatedly in His tireless love for the children of Israel.

Separated from his biological family (a family descended from Jacob, also known as Israel) as the result of an evil order from the pharaoh of Egypt, Moses was then adopted into that very same pharaoh's royal family and became a man "mighty in words and deeds" (Acts 7:22). That is God's sovereignty. Near the age of forty he witnesses one of the Israelites being beaten by an Egyptian and reacts by killing the offender. That is human responsibility. Pharaoh tries to punish Moses for this but can't because he has already fled the country. (He becomes a fugitive, just like I once was.) He marries, has children, and settles into a life of shepherding for his father-in-law.

A CAREER OF INTERCEDING FOR HIS PEOPLE

Then, in response to the passionate and persistent prayers of the sons of Israel (human responsibility), who had now been enslaved in Egypt over four hundred years, God *comes down* to deliver them and tells

Moses He is going to send him back to Pharaoh so he can lead the people out of Egypt (divine sovereignty).

So Moses begins his career of interceding for the people of Israel: first with Pharaoh and then, for the next forty years, with God.

With displays of His awesome power, God mightily delivers the people; and Moses leads the biggest and most successful jailbreak ever. A perfectly executed escape! And yet, just a few days following their miraculous deliverance, the "escapees" begin to complain and quarrel with Moses—a pattern that never seems to change.

Yes, this was a difficult group of "neighbors" God had sent Moses' way. Working with these people would be draining, discouraging, and very messy. In fact, when Moses gave his farewell address to the people, recounting all they had been through together, he told them, "You have been rebellious against the Lord from the day that I knew you" (Deut. 9:24).

So what was it that enabled Moses to endure with such people for so long? What permitted Moses to keep pressing on despite their rudeness, complaints, and outright disobedience? It was his personal knowledge of God. Forty years after fleeing Egypt, Moses had encountered God at a burning bush (see Exodus 3 and 4). It was an intense and personal meeting. And when it was over, Moses knew beyond any doubt who it was who had made him ruler and judge over his people. It was the eternal, sovereign, self-sustaining God who had a special purpose for Moses' life. God like no other god, whose name was "I AM WHO I AM" (Ex. 3:14).

What an example of God's great mercy and grace! The great I AM chose to reveal Himself to a man who had tried to serve Him and instead wound up killing someone. To the one who had fled, God gave a new beginning in the form of a history-altering assignment. What hope this is for us, dear reader! If God can work with Moses, then why not you? Why not me?

MAKING KNOWN THE GREAT I AM

Moses now understood that his main mission was not to lead the people out of Egypt for the sole purpose of obtaining their deliverance, but to make God—the great I AM—known among His people through His mighty earth-altering acts! "This is My name forever, and this is My memorial-name to all generations" (Ex. 3:15 NASB). This is the name of the one Jesus told His disciples to address in prayer. It is the name that you and I should be hallowing above all else.

Moses' intimacy with God and his motivation that God's name be glorified enabled him to persevere through the difficulties and trials, the disrespect and disobedience that would confront him over and over again the next forty years. His intimacy with God enabled him to intercede for others in bold and powerful prayers. His radical prayers resulted in radical love.

Exodus 32 through 34 record one of the darkest moments of Israel's history. And yet they also give account to one of the greatest moments of radical intercession—radical prayer and radical love—by one man for another.

The people had been gloriously delivered by God from Egypt. He had provided them manna to eat and water to drink in the wilderness. He had instructed them on how to worship and meet with Him, and had taught them how to live with one another. He did all this through Moses, who would usually go alone to meet with God either because He had called Moses or because the people had asked Moses, on their behalf, to make a request of God.

On this occasion, Moses had been called by God to meet with Him, a call that was witnessed by at least seventy people (Ex. 24:9). But this time, Moses is gone forty days and forty nights. The people think something has happened to him and that he is probably not coming back. So they ask Aaron, Moses' very own brother and one of the seventy-plus people who had witnessed the call, to "make us gods that shall go before us" (Ex. 32:1). Astonishingly, Aaron leads the people in committing high treason against the great I AM by building them a golden calf—a statue they made themselves. A statue that did not even have a name!

TREASON!

As part of this treasonous act, the people willfully misappropriated God's funds. The very gold God Himself told them to plunder from the Egyptians was now shaped into the form of an animal and became the object of their worship.

But the peoples' highest form of treason was in misappropriating God's glory. Dancing before this golden idol, the Israelites declared to each other, "This is your god, O Israel, that brought you out of the land of Egypt" (v. 4). By turning their faces to the calf, they had turned their backs on God. Instead of hallowing the name of Yahweh, they gave glory to a god whose name they did not even know.

Moses is unaware of what is happening in his absence. But God is not. He tells Moses what the people have done and is so angry that He wants to wipe out the whole nation and begin again with Moses. But instead of taking God up on the offer, Moses does four amazing things.

MOSES' BOLD INTERCESSION

First, Moses engages the angry God directly.

In most anger management classes, it is usually advised not to engage a person while he or she is enraged. We are told to give them space, let them cool down. But Moses approaches God—even after God has asked Moses to leave Him alone so He could direct His anger against the Israelites!

Second, in his engagement, Moses reminds God of what He has done and what He has said over Israel's history. He reminds God that He is the one who brought them out of Egypt. He is the one who promised Abraham, Isaac, and Jacob that their descendants would be innumerable and that they would inherit a land forever. And He is the one whose reputation would be mocked by the Egyptians if He destroyed His people.

Third, Moses makes a big, radical, and bold request, "Turn from Your fierce wrath, and relent from this harm to Your people" (v. 12). Moses intercedes for the people, making a very specific request that would be for the people's own good, but his main motivation was the glory of God. We cannot lose sight of the fact that Moses had just spent forty days and nights alone with God. This was truly a radical time-out! The result of this time was a deep intimacy with God that led to bold intercession for others. Moses prayed—and God relented.

God relented in that He did not wipe out all the people as He originally intended. However, He cannot overlook sin; and this great sin could not go unpunished. Oh, my beloved reader, do you fully understand that Yahweh does not gloss over our sin? He does not sweep it under the rug, ignore it, or call it a mistake. And He always requires a payment. The blood of three thousand men flowed (v. 28) as a consequence of this grievous sin.

After seeing their gross idolatry firsthand, Moses does a fourth mind-boggling thing. He tells the people he is going to go before the Lord to see if he could make atonement for their sin. What a beautiful illustration of what Jesus did for us! The person who was innocent was offering to make atonement for the guilty. While Moses had been bold before in asking God not to kill the people, he was even bolder this time in asking God to *forgive* them. The truly mind-boggling part of his prayer is that he ends with the request that if God would not forgive their sin, then he wanted God to remove his name from His book of the righteous (v. 32)!

Lest you think this is just an exaggerated scene from the Old Testament, look at the apostle Paul's similar declaration in Romans 9:1–5. After writing his masterful description of God's glorious grace and salvation found in Christ alone (Rom. 1–8), Paul expresses great sorrow over his unbelieving kinsmen. Like Moses, Paul had an intimate relationship with God which resulted in an overflowing love for others. Like Moses, he cries out, "For I could wish that I myself were accursed and cut off from Christ for the sake of my brothers" (Rom. 9:3 esv).

God's reply to Moses' second prayer is not as clear as it was to his first prayer. Here Moses' specific request was for God to forgive the people of their sin. God responds that whoever has sinned will be blotted out of His book. He postpones punishment for a future time, but reiterates that sin will be punished. In this we see that while Moses was a type of savior, he could never be *the* savior. Although Moses was innocent of this particular sin he was, nevertheless, a sinner. There was no way he could make atonement for the sins of the people. One who is greater than Moses was needed, and that one is Christ Jesus, God's only Son.

What should be our response when God does not answer our prayers in the way we had hoped? Submission. Submission is only possible in relationships where there is trust. Trust is only possible in relationships where there is consistent intimacy. Moses had consistent intimacy with God; therefore, he could trust Him. Because Moses trusted God, he could submit to Him.

God then tells Moses it is time for him to move

the people on toward the Promised Land. In an act of great grace, God promises to drive out all the nations that would be in their way. Yet He told Moses that He would not go with them, lest His anger destroy the people (Ex. 33:2–3).

It is not clear how long Moses waited before he came again to God with another request. But we do know he came. And once again, he fueled his prayer with God's own words.

Moses reminded God that He Himself had told Moses that he has favor in His sight; and God knows Moses by name (vv. 16–17). In other words, Moses reminds God of their intimate relationship. He also reminds God that all the rest of the people were His people, too (vv. 12–13). Once again, Moses is bold and radical. He tells God that if He will not go with them, he does not want to move. Appealing to God's reputation even beyond the children of Israel, Moses asks, "How else will the nations know that we belong to You if You do not go with us?" (v. 16 paraphrased).

Because of the great sin of idolatry, Moses made three bold and radical requests of the Lord: Don't destroy us! Forgive us! Go with us! His intercessions on behalf of the people rose from petitions concerning their physical well-being to petitions concerning their spiritual well-being. What good would it be for the children of Israel to have a land flowing with milk and honey, to have comfort and security, if they did not have God Himself?

God responds favorably to Moses' request. Exodus 33:17 says, "So the Lord said to Moses, 'I will also do this thing that you have spoken; for you have found grace in My sight, and I know you by name.'" Truly, God was gracious. He gave them another set of tablets containing the Law to replace those that had been broken. When the tabernacle was completed, just as He had commanded, His glory filled the tent so intensely that Moses was not able to enter. God's presence was with His people—and He would accompany them into the Promised Land. The last verse of Exodus tell us, "For the cloud of the Lord was above the tabernacle by day, and fire was over it by night, in the sight of all the house of Israel, throughout all their journeys."

Moses prayed—and God moved.

———

My friend, I humbly ask you: Do you have the intimacy with God that leads to a loving passion for others? First John 4:8 says, "He who does not love does not know God, for God is love." This is one way in which we can do a practical inventory of our progress as believers. Am I growing in my love for others? If not, then

I am most likely not growing in my love for God.

I urge you to take a radical time-out and wrestle with God our Father. Ask Him to open the eyes of your heart to see Him, to grow in your knowledge of and intimacy with the Father, Son, and Holy Spirit. Ask Him to reveal Himself to you in order that you may validate your love for Him by loving your neighbor. If you do so, I can assure you that your joy will be uncontainable, inexpressible, and full of glory (1 Peter 1:8).

Pray radically to love radically.

8

RADICAL PRAYER IN ACTION

God my Father, please grant me a fresh and unprecedented unction of Your Spirit so I can continually proclaim the "freeing" truth of Jesus Christ and the power of His love with clarity. So may I see "biblical revival" break out in prisons across America—all for the growth of the church of Jesus Christ and for the hallowing of Your holy name. ¡Aleluya! In Jesus' name, Amen.

WHAT I FOUND TO BE TRUE in Moses' life was true in mine. That is, as I grew in my intimacy with the Lord, I grew in my love for others. I made it my prayer that God would give me a heart for Him and for others. A heart like Moses' and the apostle Paul's.

As mentioned earlier, during the first twenty-one years of our ministry, we had focused almost exclusively on post-prison ministry, helping Christian inmates transition from prison back to society. Then at the end of 2011, the Lord opened the doors for more in-prison ministry through our Freedom God's Way weekends.

It would have been easy to make a shift from

focusing exclusively on post-prison ministry to in-prison ministry. There truly is a genuine hunger and thirst for truth among America's inmates; a hunger that only the Lord Jesus can satisfy. It is also true that His church has been designed as the only vehicle for meeting that need. America's prisons are, as Jesus says in John 4:35, a field "white for harvest."

But there were also subtle dangers that could lead us, wrongly, to make this ministry shift. There is a certain "glamor" in going inside a prison, especially those with notorious reputations. It is tempting to issue reports to donors stating that we preached to so many hundreds of inmates, conducted X-number of services in Y-number of prisons, and saw Z-number of men and women make decisions for Christ.

Post-prison ministry, however, is far less glamorous. To be effective long term, such ministry needs to be done with smaller numbers of people at a time. It takes hard work to walk beside someone as they grow in the Lord while facing the challenges of finding a place to live, securing employment and transportation, and establishing healthy relationships with friends and family. It can be a lot like Moses' experience with the children of Israel. It can be messy and risky.

Barbara and I, along with our board members, began to pray and wait upon the Lord to see what He would do, what doors He would either open or close. The board made the hard decision to suspend operation of the residential part of our ministry while we took time to review how best to help someone upon their release from prison. While we no longer conducted discipleship in a family-like setting, we were still working with local churches through our Meet Me at the Gate™ initiative and a Thursday night Bible study. (Barbara described this Bible study group as "five guys and a box of pizza." Tom Horton took on the responsibility for this study and faithfully led the group each week.)

"GOD, SURPRISE US!"

At the beginning of 2012, Barbara and I began asking God to show us what He would like to do with Thursday nights. I would literally pray, "God, surprise us! Show us something that only You can do!" He sent a few more men. At the same time, a recently released woman we had interacted with at a Freedom God's Way weekend asked if she too could attend the study. At first we hesitated because for years it had only been for men. But we soon agreed, prompted by the fact that she would be driven to the study by another woman— thus giving us two new members! And by this time, Barbara was herself attending, preparing an occasional home-cooked meal as a change from the usual pizza.

A few weeks later, we were contacted by two wives whose husbands were incarcerated. Their husbands had attended a Freedom God's Way weekend, told their wives about our ministry, and suggested they contact us. Very soon, we had four more people attending Thursday nights—the two wives attending in person and their husbands attending via cellphones, listening in to the study from prison.

Next a sister started attending in person, with her brother calling in from prison. These were followed by two area detectives who had been arrested for alleged illegal activities conducted while carrying out their undercover police work. Since they were codefendants and not allowed to have contact with one another, they would have to take turns attending in person. (This was a detail we had never had to think about before, making sure two people did *not* show up on the same night!)

Barbara and I began to share the teaching responsibilities. We added singing and times of testimony to the evening. A retired missionary couple who was now residing in the Koinonia House as temporary caretakers, along with our social media consultant and his wife, helped with preparing and serving the dinner each week. A woman who had contacted us for help with her post-prison ministry in Maine began attending via

telephone, as did a young man from Colorado who had
been incarcerated at a county jail for sixteen months.

THE ONE CONSTANT: PRAYER

Each week it seemed there was someone different.
But there was one constant: Prayer. All during the evening, at different times and in different formats, there
would be prayer.

We prayed for God to provide housing, employment, transportation, and healing of broken relationships. We asked God to circumcise our hearts, cutting
away those sins that were hindering us from experiencing the fullness of life that Jesus offers. As we prayed,
we experienced the great range of emotions that come
when we "rejoice with those who rejoice and weep
with those who weep" (Rom. 12:15). One moment we
would jump for joy with praise to God for a victory He
had brought about in someone's life; the next, we would
be weeping with one who was enduring the deep pain
of wounds caused by their own or someone else's sin.
We prayed—and God moved.

A RADICAL TIME OUT

Attendance on Thursday nights had grown to
the point where we had outgrown Koinonia House.
We needed to find a new location—and a new name.

Radical Time Out (RTO) was a name we had used for a brief time several years earlier when we had tried to start a similar ministry. Now it seemed the perfect description for what was happening. We were being "radical," going back to the root of God's Word. We were taking a "time out" from our usual schedules to learn more about God Himself and how we could hallow His holy name together. As I like to say, we were taking a time-out to consult the playbook and listen to the coach so we could execute the plays He wanted us to make.

When we moved the meeting to a local church, our attendance continued to grow. This brought a new challenge—how exactly to provide a healthy dinner each week. We prayed and God moved by sending us Dominick and Mary, a couple whose daughter was incarcerated. In God's sovereignty, Barbara had spoken to them the night they first attended RTO and found out Dominick was a semi-retired chef.

Within two weeks, our new "chef" and his wonderful wife began their ministry of preparing dinner for our RTO family, which now included more wives of incarcerated husbands, parents of children in prison, people facing possible criminal charges, those awaiting trial or sentencing or on probation, and those coming back to society after more than twenty years of incarceration. In addition, we were joined by prison ministry volunteers and those who were simply looking to experience God's radical grace.

Today, Radical Time Out continues to grow, and is a place where the Gospel continues to mightily transcend color, class, culture, and crime.

Bill and his wife Terry had relocated to Illinois and were in the early stages of finding a church and establishing new Christian friendships when Bill was introduced to our ministry. He began attending Radical Time Out. He also started to attend a men's prayer group that met on Wednesdays at noon at the Koinonia House, a group that grew out of RTO. These men gather specifically to pray for their children.

About this same time, Bill and Terry were visiting with family and recognized that their nephew Erik was spiraling toward self-destruction. Near the end of high school, Erik started to hang around people who used marijuana, and it was not long before he too was using it. The power of sin increased its hold on Erik. While away from home on a trip, Erik's father died suddenly from a heart attack. Erik was devastated. The memory of one of the last conversations he had with his father was particularly unsettling. Just three days before his death, Erik's father had told him, with tears, "Give your heart to the Lord."

RADICAL PRAYERS FOR ERIK

But Erik did not turn to God. He fell deeper into a lifestyle of selling drugs and unhealthy relationships. He left home. He was involved in illegal activities and soon found himself in the county jail for six weeks during the Christmas season. Things did not change. Erik suffered from anxiety, loneliness, and the lack of a father figure and good friends. "I was always looking over my shoulder," he would later recall.

Of course, Bill and Terry had been praying for Erik as concerned uncle and aunt. After their family visit, their prayers intensified. They asked their small groups at church and the dads at Koinonia House to join in crying out for the Lord to redeem their nephew.

As they prayed radically, they began to love radically. They arranged for Erik to move in with their son, who was in campus ministry near Detroit. But Erik soon fell back into his old ways. He even had an automobile accident in his cousin's car that he had borrowed without permission.

Bill and Terry continued to pray for Erik's salvation and continued to love. This time they arranged for him to live with them. They encouraged him to attend church and Radical Time Out with them, praying also that he would develop positive friendships. One night Erik told Bill and Terry he was going to attend a party with a girl he had met through social media. When the girl arrived at their home to pick up Erik, she met his aunt and uncle. She told them she was a student at an area Christian college. They were suspicious, yet reluctantly they let Erik leave with her.

In a moment that illustrates prayer's divine dance between God's sovereignty and human responsibility, the Holy Spirit moved Bill to pray for Erik's safety. This is one of the mysteries of prayer and a tension believers need to embrace. God knew Erik was in danger and had the power to deliver him from the situation. Why then did Bill need to pray? Bill needed to pray so that Bill could know God cares and is involved in the details of his life.

In obedience to the Holy Spirit's prompting, Bill prayed—and God moved. Within moments of praying, Erik called his uncle from the party, and Bill asked a specific question for which Erik had no answer. "Is the girl really a college student?" This time, the Holy Spirit would not let Erik lie. Bill said, "Come on home, Erik," which he did, feeling guilty and defeated.

The next evening, Erik attended RTO by himself. Barbara was teaching on forgiveness and used a video to conclude her message. It told the story of the freedom from bitterness that a Christian mother experienced when she forgave the young drunk driver who had killed her teenaged daughter. God used the mother to bring the young man to find freedom in Christ for the forgiveness of his sins. The young man's name was Eric.

GRACE EXTENDED

Erik watched, heard his name in the video, and knew. "It was a message meant for me. I broke down at my table," Erik later recounted. "This was the grace of God that is extended to me and everyone." A few of the women at his table at RTO prayed with Erik. He repented of his sin and confessed faith in Christ Jesus as his Lord and Savior. Someone asked Erik to share with the whole group what had just happened. In tears, he told them he had just taken the advice that, three years before, his father had given him.

As this book goes to press, it has been about a year since Erik's conversion. At first he was frustrated by unsuccessful attempts to find employment, but the Lord later provided Erik a job that has been perfect for him—teaching soccer to youngsters. He was accepted into junior college and offered financial support. He now surrounds himself with friends who are also believers, friends from church and RTO. They continue to pray radically for Erik and *with* Erik.

Since experiencing grace for himself, Erik says it

is now easier for him to extend grace to others. He is at peace with his life and no longer looking over his shoulder. But the radical prayers for him continue, now mingled with his own.

His uncle Bill still prays boldly for him. He writes, "Today my bold prayers are for God to work through Erik in extraordinary ways, ways I can only imagine, but God already knows. Will God empower Erik to share his testimony boldly with others? Will he begin to teach or counsel those who are struggling and broken? Will he lead someone to Christ? Will Erik someday be a loving, encouraging, and forgiving father, modeling his faith to his own children? Those are radical prayers of *expectancy* by those around him! We can pray, thanking God in advance, for everything He will do in Erik's life in the years ahead!"

Through the ministry of Radical Time Out we are now building bridges and restoring hope by teaching the Word of God, connecting individuals to local churches, and above all hallowing God's holy name through biblical, radical prayer.

9

RADICAL REDEMPTION

Hear my deep cry, my Lord, as I honor and call on Your holy and loving name alone, even as Jesus and the Holy Spirit intercede before Your holy throne for me. I love Your truth. I desire Your shalom—Your peaceful presence—more than the water I drink and the air I breathe. I beg of You, grant me my radical desire to experience Your glory so that I might worship and adore You more. I am Yours alone. Fill me with Your glory so I would reflect that glory for all to see.
In Jesus' name, Amen.

FROM MY STUDY OF JESUS' teaching to the disciples (Luke 11) I learned that the emphatic hallowing, or honoring, of God's holy name should be the supreme focus of my prayers. From my study of Moses, I learned how intimacy in communion with God the Father would result in a boldness in praying for others—including difficult, obstinate, and rebellious people. My lesson for praying precise, specific prayers, however, was impressed on me through the study of a British preacher.

George Whitefield became a true follower of Christ when he was twenty years old. Upon his conversion, he wrote that he had found a new delight in Bible reading and a rich joy in prayer, resulting in "the multitude of peace." Arnold A. Dallimore, in his biography of Whitefield, wrote, "He not only spent the hour from 4 till 5 in the morning in communion with God, but he lived in the spirit of prayer throughout the day, and prayer proved indeed his 'native air.'"[1]

In 1737, at age twenty-three, Whitefield accepted the invitation of John Wesley to join him in his missionary endeavors in the American colony of Georgia. Georgia had been recently established in order to give people released from England's debtors' prisons a place to live.

I felt an immediate connection with this eighteenth-century preacher. Like Whitefield, I lived in Georgia when I first came to America; and we were both involved in ministry to those just released from prison.

FOUR QUALITIES FOR EFFECTIVE MINISTRY

Leaving the comforts of London and undertaking a dangerous Atlantic crossing, Whitefield prayed, "God, give me a deep humility, a well-guided zeal, a burning love and a single eye."[2]

142

In Whitefield's radical prayer, I find the qualities needed for effective service for Christ. Whitefield's four petitions provide a synopsis of the essence of Jesus' earthly ministry.

1. Jesus exhibited *deep humility* by acknowledging (especially in His high priestly prayer in John 17) that, although one with the Father Himself, He was the sent one, and His mission was to carry out the Father's instructions.

2. Jesus demonstrated that *His passion (zeal)* was well-guided by appropriately controlling His human emotions. He displayed anger when justified (for example, at the cleansing of His Father's temple), yet exercised great self-control in both His wilderness temptation and enduring the humiliations of His trial and crucifixion.

3. Jesus displayed *His burning love* both for His Father in heaven and for those the Father had given Him to secure for an eternal future with Him.

4. Jesus understood that *His "single eye"* — His great purpose while on earth — was

His Father's glory (John 17:1). He knew
that in order to vindicate the holy name
of God the Father, He would need to
suffer the great agonies of the cross and
even death itself.

To this precise prayer for *a deep humility, a well-
guided zeal, a burning love*, and *a single eye*, Whitefield
added one final declaration: "and then let men or devils
do their worst."[3] Whitefield was completely confident
that when God the Father granted him his four petitions, he could face any battle, any difficulty, any hard-
ship in ministry that might come his way.

And come they did! Even before reaching Georgia,
Whitefield almost died from a fever that was ravag-
ing those on the ship. He endured great storms at sea
during his trips across the Atlantic. He suffered attacks
and criticisms launched by other clergymen uncomfortable with his messages and methodologies. He even
received threats of assassination.

History reveals that God the Father was pleased
to grant this young man a deep humility, a well-guided
zeal, a burning love, and a single eye; and gave him thirty-
two years of ministry during which he impacted his
world for Christ. Dallimore concludes his biography of
Whitefield by stating:

But as Bishop Ryle says, "Whitefield was entirely chief and first among the English Reformers of the 18th century." He initiated almost all of its enterprises—the open-air preaching, the use of lay preachers, the publishing of a magazine, the organizing of an association, and the holding of a conference. And by his thirteen crossings of the ocean, he provided the international scope of the movement. Among his accomplishments there must be recognized the host of men and women he led to Jesus Christ and the large part he played in this great work of revival on both sides of the Atlantic.[4]

Our world needs more believers like Whitefield. We need a host of Christians to engage in radical, biblical—and precise—prayer. We need millions more who will pray for God the Father's name to be hallowed throughout the world. We need tens of millions more who will seek the power of the Holy Spirit in order to be changed into the likeness of Christ.

O, beloved reader, will you take a radical time-out just now and join me in prayer:

Our father and our God, grant my reader and me "a deep humility, a well-guided zeal, a burning love and a single eye, and then let men or devils do their worst." In Jesus' matchless name. Amen.

SHELBY AND ME

Shelby Arabie is an articulate, handsome, and extremely gifted man. Given a set of tools and the raw materials, Shelby can build anything with a motor and keep it running in top condition. His interest in keeping all kinds of machines running smoothly spills over into his physical life as well. Adhering to a healthy diet, he maintains a strict exercise regimen.

The first time I met him (before my conviction by the Spirit at a friend's cabin), Shelby and I had virtually nothing in common on which to build a friendship. The one thing we did share was a common acquaintance, Burl Cain, warden of the Louisiana State Penitentiary at Angola.

I was doing ministry at Angola when I met Shelby in late 2002. At the time, Shelby was a thirty-nine-year-old inmate who had been incarcerated for seventeen years. Having earned the highest trustee status an inmate can achieve, Shelby worked as the head mechanic and machinist for the warden. His workshop was located directly behind the Ranch House, the gathering place for visitors on the prison grounds outside of the fenced-in compounds.

Work assignments at the Ranch House are coveted positions. Not only are these inmates able to go on "the other side of the fence," but they can interact at times with the warden's guests. Unlike most of the trustees who look forward to these opportunities to relate to "free people" (whether just for the pleasure of someone new to talk to or with self-promoting interests in mind), Shelby kept his distance, especially if he heard the visitors were Christians. He thought of Christians as weak people and hypocrites. From the start, Shelby made it clear to me that he had no time for God; in fact, he was not even sure God existed.

The following summer, I was able to bring my daughter Cesia, my wife Barbara, and our two sons, Howard and Kenneth, on what would be their first of many trips to Angola. In March 2004, Barbara and the boys returned with me for a whole week, participating each evening in services throughout the different prison camps.

During the day, while I ministered one-on-one or with small groups of inmates, Barbara made sure the boys kept up with their schoolwork at the Ranch House. It was not difficult to motivate them to get their homework done since the trustees had plenty of interesting things to show my "city" boys.

For the next few years, their reward for doing their studies while at Angola included lessons on how to hunt frogs, skin wild boar, trap raccoons, and drive golf carts and ATVs. At this first visit, we did not know of Shelby's gift for teaching and were somewhat surprised that he was the one with whom the boys connected.

In the evening services, I was showing a powerful music video featuring Nicole C. Mullen singing "My Redeemer Lives" as background to the video of Team Hoyt, a father-son team that competes in triathlons. Team Hoyt consists of a quadriplegic adult son who had a desire to participate in the famous Ironman triathlon in Hawaii and his father, already at an age when most men are beginning to slow down. The dad trained for each of the events and designed apparatuses that allowed him to swim, bike, and run while pulling, pushing, and carrying his disabled son.

TEAM HOYT AND A RADICAL REQUEST

When Shelby returned to his dorm within the prison compound one night, he heard the inmates talking about the amazing story of Team Hoyt. The next day he asked Barbara to see the video. Thinking he was interested because he was a runner, Barbara soon learned Shelby was really interested because his older brother Stephen had sustained a brain injury that left him severely limited in his speech, thinking, and movement.

Watching the video with the boys and Shelby in his workshop is a moment Barbara will not soon forget. She realized God was opening a special door of friendship; a little crack was forming in his hardened heart. Although I would bring hundreds of visitors to Angola over the next several years, I was very selective of those I would take back to meet Shelby. His friendship with me and my family was precious, and I guarded it carefully, for the glory of God.

Soon after my personal revival experience at the cabin, I began to pray persistently for an "impossible" radical prayer request, Shelby's conversion to Christ. Although Barbara and I had been praying for this since 2003, I now became more precise and more intentional in my prayers for Shelby.

Not long afterwards, in August 2011, Shelby was granted a hearing before the Louisiana Pardon Board. This was a big deal! In a state known for its harsh sentencing, for an offender with a second-degree murder conviction to be given a hearing before the board was a rare occurrence indeed! Shelby asked the Hortons and me to appear on his behalf at the hearing in Baton Rouge.

Although Shelby was not a believer in Jesus, I had no problem supporting his pardon. His story is truly a textbook case of a prisoner "rehabilitation." His arrest had come as a twenty-one-year-old, when Shelby had worked full-time as an electrical lineman, yet occasionally was "supplementing" his income by selling marijuana. One night he and a friend arranged a purchase with two other men. But those others had a different plan. They assaulted Shelby and his friend, tied them up, and stole about ten pounds of pot with a street value of $9,000. Shelby and his partner managed to free themselves. They pursued the men and eventually caught up with them. Shelby fired one shot, killing one of the men. He was arrested, convicted, and sentenced to life in prison.

In Louisiana, all life sentences are handed down without the possibility of parole. Therefore, without any hope and after two years imprisoned at one facility, Shelby managed to escape to the Florida Keys for almost four months. Once captured, he was sent to Angola. As punishment for the escape, he spent the next four years in "confined cell restriction," locked up twenty-three hours each day in an eight- by ten-foot cell. It was there that he decided to improve himself, each day running miles in place and reading voraciously.

Upon returning to the general population, he became a "model prisoner," continuously seeking to improve himself—even becoming one of sixteen ASE (Automotive Service Excellence) technicians in the world to possess all fifty-one active certifications. He helped the warden establish, and became an instructor for, a vocational-technical program for the younger offenders at Angola. When Hurricane Katrina devastated New Orleans in 2005, Shelby was entrusted to be part of a select crew assigned to repair the city's damaged water pumps!

Six years after that deadly hurricane and now age forty-eight, Shelby clearly was no threat; I knew he would certainly become a contributing member of society if given the chance.

The Hortons and I traveled to Angola a few days before the parole board hearing. We wanted to meet with Shelby and remind him that only God our Father could free him both from Angola and from the guilt of his sin. Although there were several influential people working on his behalf, only God was able to change hearts and minds, first of the five members of the parole board and then of the state governor.

I had asked Shelby a few times over the years if I could pray with him. He would always politely refuse.

But now I had been praying Exodus 34:10 for him, where Yahweh said, "Behold, I make a covenant. Before all your people I will do marvels such as have not been done in all the earth, nor in any nation; and all the people among whom you are shall see the work of the Lord. For it is an awesome thing that I will do with you." This time, when the Hortons and I asked Shelby to pray with us, he agreed. Inside, we were silently rejoicing as we saw another crack appear in his hardened heart. God the Holy Spirit, was at work.

PRECISE IN PRAYER

To his face, I boldly told him that God would act, not because of him, but because we were coming to God on his behalf. As long as he denied God, he would have no access to Him. However, because of our love for Shelby, the Hortons and I would continue to pursue God on his behalf.

With my newly acquired habit of being precise in prayer, I asked God the Father to grant Shelby three things. First, that the pardon board would recommend a reduction of his sentence from life to forty-five years, thereby making Shelby eligible for immediate parole because he had already served more than 60 percent of that time. Second, that the vote would not just be the needed supermajority to pass (four out of five votes), but rather be a unanimous vote. This way there would be no doubt that God was the one moving in the members' hearts and minds. Third, that the governor would act quickly and favorably upon the recommendation of the pardon board.

The Hortons and I, along with Shelby's family and other supporters, including the victim's daughter, were present with the pardon board in Baton Rouge. Shelby appeared via a live video feed from Angola. After hearing testimony, including from Shelby himself taking full responsibility for the victim's murder, it took the board less than five minutes to unanimously vote in favor of reducing his sentence to forty-five years. We erupted in shouts of joy! Two of our three requests had been graciously provided for by our heavenly Father!

Later the next day, when we were able to return to Angola and see Shelby, he told us that God had awakened him at 4:00 a.m. the day of the hearing and had given him a tremendous peace and assurance about his meeting with the board. To me, this was an example of Ephesians 3:20: God going beyond what we asked and giving Shelby a personal assurance that He cared for Shelby and had His hand on him. It was also quite an admission from someone who used to tell me he did not know if God even existed.

THE GOVERNOR ACTS

It took almost two years for the governor to act on the recommendation of the pardon board, which may seem like God did not grant us our third petition. However, this needs to be put in perspective. Between 2008 and mid-2011, of the four hundred fifty recommendations sent by the board to the governor, he acted on only seventy-two of them. Thirty-six were rejected and thirty-six were approved. Of those approved, only one of those involved someone who was still in prison.

Two years was a "quick" response, and more importantly, it was favorable. By the grand providence of God, Barbara and I had arrived at Angola the night before the governor announced his decision. Months before we had arranged to bring the chairman of the board of Wheaton College, Dr. David Gieser, along with his wife Mary, to see firsthand where Wheaton College students had been spending their spring break in ministry for the last ten years. On July 12, 2013, the governor made a rare commutation, accepting the pardon board's recommendation and reducing Shelby's sentence from life to forty-five years. God gave us the joy of celebrating this news with Shelby in person! A few days later, after serving twenty-nine years of his sentence, Shelby was released from Angola. God had graciously granted him one kind of freedom.

Nineteen months later, Barbara and I were once again headed to Angola. On our way, we hoped to see Shelby for the first time outside of Angola and called to invite him to dinner. Barbara spoke to him while I drove and at first it sounded as though Shelby was being hesitant—as if he wasn't interested in talking or meeting with us. But soon he was inviting us for dinner and insisting we spend the night at his home rather than a hotel!

OUR DINNER WITH SHELBY

During dinner, Shelby explained his hesitancy on the phone by saying he was only trying to figure out how to rearrange his evening's schedule in order to make time to see us.

So here we were at his home. And no sooner did we finish dinner than he took us to meet his beloved brother Stephen. We watched Shelby lovingly care for Stephen, staying until Stephen's overnight caregiver arrived. We prayed with Stephen before leaving and then headed over to Shelby's place of employment.

It was late in the evening when he took us for a tour of the machine shop and recounted the successes he was having. He had secured his first position within four days of his release, had been promoted, and was now developing a training center so the company could offer skilled technicians to service the generators they manufactured for use on the oil rigs in the Gulf of Mexico.

To say Barbara and I were impressed would be sheer understatement.

But the best news we heard that memorable evening was Shelby's profession that he believed that Jesus Christ was the Messiah and the Lord of his life. He gave Christ all the credit for all he had accomplished in life and acknowledged that God had not released him from prison one day sooner than he was ready.

God had graciously given Shelby a second gift of freedom—delivery from His wrath and eternal hell!

As Barbara and I went to sleep that night, she started to laugh with joy and asked, "Are we really spending the night in Shelby Arabie's bed? I'm not sure if this is what most people think of when they read Jesus' promise of an abundant life in John 10:10, but it is for me!"

And by the way, because Shelby used to transport an exercise bike for me to whatever accommodations I had in the prison, I would joke with him that I could only stay at his place if he had a fitness center. He said he had a gym at home, where he worked out each morning and I was welcome to join him at his regular time—2:30 a.m.!

Actually, I did join him in the gym at 2:30 the next morning. (After only a couple hours sleep!) And later that evening, I had the great privilege of telling the men of Angola what I had just heard, seen, and experienced with Shelby: A radical answer to a radical prayer for the hallowing of God our Father's holy name. To that I say only one word. *¡Aleluya!*

10

READY TO
BE RADICAL?

*My gracious heavenly Father, grant me a
heart that will take heed of Moses' last words
to Your people: That I would observe carefully
all that You command me. I acknowledge
that Your words are not empty, they are not
idle. Indeed, they are my very life. Use Your
Word and Your Spirit to ignite in me a deeper,
greater, burning desire to hallow Your
name in all of my prayers.
In Jesus' name, Amen.*

SO, WHAT DO I MEAN by a radical, biblical prayer?
Once again, Moses provides an example in his encounter with God in Exodus 34:1–17.

RADICAL PRAYER: TOTAL SURRENDER

God graciously relented from destroying the Hebrews when they committed high treason against Him
by building the golden calf and attributing to it—and
not Yahweh—their miraculous deliverance from Egypt.
God called Moses to come up Mount Sinai and receive a replacement set of stone tablets containing His

covenant with the people. He also responded to Moses' greatest prayer, "Please, show me Your glory" (Ex. 33:18), by descending in a cloud, passing by Moses, and making a powerful proclamation of His character: "The Lord, the Lord God, merciful and gracious, long-suffering, and abounding in goodness and truth, keeping mercy for thousands, forgiving iniquity and transgression and sin, by no means clearing the guilty, visiting the iniquity of the fathers upon the children and the children's children to the third and fourth generation" (Ex. 34:6–7).

Together, this magnificent moment marked Israel's new beginning.

A radical, biblical prayer is one that begins with a correct understanding and careful acknowledgment of whose presence we are entering. When we pray, we are addressing the eternal, self-sustaining, sovereign King of the universe; and we can do so only through Jesus Christ, His Son. Moses' physical posture demonstrated his understanding of God's mercy and grace. Verse 8 tells us that "Moses made haste and bowed his head toward the earth, and worshiped"; he assumed a posture of total surrender and gave reverence to Jehovah for Jehovah's sake. No requesting, no demanding. Purely worshiping.

My beloved reader, I encourage you to try, if you are physically able, to assume a posture of surrender during your private prayer times. Yes, we can pray to God in any position. But how many of us are guilty of praying from casual positions which lend themselves to drifting thoughts or even sleep? A posture of surrender encourages alertness and attentiveness. A posture of surrender encourages true worship.

RADICAL PRAYER: HONEST CONFESSION

When Moses does speak to God, he begins with an honest confession: "If now I have found grace in Your sight, O Lord, let my Lord, I pray, go among us, even though we are a stiff-necked people; and pardon our iniquity and our sin" (Ex. 34:9).

A radical, biblical prayer is one that is made with an honest confession of our own sinful state and with an understanding that prayer is only possible because of God's great grace. There should be no hint of entitlement or an attitude of "I deserve this" in our prayers. Rather, we come before Jehovah in deep humility and with an overwhelming sense of gratitude, understanding that because we are sinners we do not deserve anything from Him. Yet, because He is full of grace, we are free to come.

RADICAL PRAYER:
SELFLESS SERVITUDE

Not only did Moses ask Jehovah to go among them, he asked God to "take us as Your inheritance" (v. 9). Notice Moses did not ask for something material, such as food or wealth, or even for position. At this moment in the young nation's history, it would have been natural for Moses to ask, "Go among us and give us the land You promised our forefathers." But he did not. Instead, he made an astonishing request, recalling the Lord's words from Exodus 19:5, that of all the peoples on the earth, they would be His special treasure, His own possession.

A radical, biblical prayer is one that expresses delight in being owned by God. We should come into the presence of God fully satisfied in being His treasure. What good is it to have an abundance of wealth and power in this life if our souls will be separated from God for all eternity? Knowing we are His treasure brings us confidence and security. We come delighting not just in the knowledge that *we know God*, but that *God knows us*. We can delight in being His bond-servants, as the apostle Paul described himself, because we know for certain that God is a good and trustworthy master.

RADICAL PRAYER: EAGER EXPECTANCY

As a demonstration of His crazy love for His people, God answers Moses' request with an over-the-top response. He says that not only will He go with them and take them as His treasure, but He promises to do "marvels such as have not been done in all the earth" (v. 10). Imagine! This statement was made to the man who had seen ten demonstrations of God's mighty power over the supposed gods of Egypt, and then watched Him miraculously part the Red Sea as an avenue for their escape. Even with all these, God was now telling Moses he could expect MORE!

A radical, biblical prayer is one of expectancy. We come acknowledging that we do not deserve anything from God. Yet, we come knowing that He delights in lavishing His love upon His children and bringing glory to Himself through amazing displays of His power. Spurgeon eloquently challenged his congregation:

> Nothing pleases God so much as when a sinner comes again very soon with twice as large a petition—"Lord thou didst hear me last time, and now I am come again." Faith is a mighty grace, and always grows upon that which it feeds. When God has heard prayer for one thing, faith comes and asks for two

things, and when God has given those two things, faith asks for six. Faith can scale the walls of heaven. She is a giant grace. She takes mountains by their roots, and puts them on other mountains, and so climbs to the throne in confidence with large petitions, knowing that she shall not be refused. We are most of us too slow to go to God. We are not like the beggars who come to the door twenty times if you do not give them anything. But if we have been heard once, we go away, instead of coming time after time, and each time with a larger prayer. Make your petitions longer and longer. Ask for ten, and if God gives them, then for a thousand, and keep going on until at last you will positively get faith enough to ask, if it were proper, as great a favor as Moses did—"I beseech thee, show me thy glory."[1]

RADICAL PRAYER: COMMITTED OBEDIENCE

We cannot lose sight, however, that when we come to God in prayer we are coming into the presence of one who is holy, unlike any other. With the words "observe what I command you" and "take heed to yourself," Jehovah commands Moses with strong action words to destroy, break, and cut down the idols of the people in the land where they were going so that they would not fall again into the trap of idolatry.

A radical, biblical prayer is one made with an unwavering commitment to obey all that God commands, for the hallowing of His holy name. We commit to worshiping no other god, "for the Lord, whose name is Jealous, is a jealous God" (Ex. 34:14).

What does it mean, that God's name is Jealous? The New Geneva Study Bible has a helpful note at Exodus 20:5, the first time in Scripture God uses such a name. "When used of God, this word describes His passion for His holy name, a zeal that demands the exclusive devotion of His people. It is employed when that claim is threatened by other deities."

My beloved reader, we are right back where we began—at the hallowing of God's holy name! What idols are there in your life that should be destroyed, broken, or cut down? What stands in your way of being obedient to all that God commands you? If you feel that your prayer life is not all that it ought to be, consider whether you are praying with an unwavering commitment to obedience. "By this we know that we love the children of God, when we love God and keep His commandments. For this is the love of God, that we keep His commandments. And His commandments are not burdensome" (1 John 5:2–3).

A FINAL LESSON FROM MOSES

Moses spent his final forty years leading a group of very difficult people from Egypt to the Promised Land. He spoke to the people on behalf of God, and he spoke to God on behalf of the people. He was a man of God; one whom the Lord knew "face to face" (Ex. 33:11). Yet, he fell into sin.

Numbers 20:1–13 records the sad account of Moses losing his temper when the people complained to him and his brother, Aaron, because they had no water in the wilderness. Assuming the role of provider of the water, and disobeying Jehovah's clear command to "speak to the rock before their eyes," Moses instead struck the rock twice. Although God was gracious in still providing water for the people and the animals, he handed down a serious consequence to both Aaron and Moses. Their ministry would be coming to an end, and neither one would be entering into the Promised Land. Their sin? "You did not believe Me, to hallow Me in the eyes of the children of Israel" (Num. 20:12; cf. Deut. 32:51). Moses and Aaron had no "do over" on this one. Although God showed them both great mercy, He did not give them the grace of a second chance. He was merciful in not giving them what they deserved right then and there: instant death. Yet He did not graciously give them something they did not deserve: the privilege of entering the Promised Land.

No wonder when Jesus taught the disciples how to pray, He began by saying, "When you pray, say: Our Father in heaven, hallowed be Your name" (Luke 11:2). Jesus' life clearly demonstrated that His main purpose was to hallow His Father's name in all that He did. He came to vindicate His Father's holy reputation through His life, death, and resurrection. Beloved reader, we must take the hallowing of God's name extremely seriously. God declared, through the prophet Isaiah, "I am the Lord, that is My name; and My glory I will not give to another" (Isa. 42:8).

When we fail to render to God our Father His hallowing through our prayers, we essentially are praying to some other god. If we are not seeking His provision alone, we are seeking it in someone or something else. This is idolatry and adultery, and God will not tolerate it.

MEETING WITH THE KING

In my ministry, I occasionally interact with government officials. Getting an audience with such people is almost never easy. We need to persist through layers of staff with phone calls and emails, consulting of calendars, scheduling appointments and often rescheduling them. And then, when we actually land on a connection point, we need to prioritize our concerns, determining which items will be put on the agenda and which will be left off.

During the meeting (when it actually happens!), we look for clues of attentiveness and hope we are being heard. When our allotted time is ended, we leave to begin waiting for an official response.

The marvelous good news for Christians is this is not the case with the King of the universe! When we believe that Jesus is the Son of God who paid the penalty for our sin through His death, burial, and resurrection, the Bible tells us that we receive the gift of Christ's righteousness. This right standing before God allows us now to come boldly and confidently before His throne of grace (Heb. 4:16) as much-beloved children approaching a much-beloved father.

There are no appointments to be made. We have an immediate audience at any time. There are no limited agendas or time constraints. We can speak to our Father about anything and everything for as long as it takes. There is no making our request through one who has no authority. Rather, we can communicate directly with the most high and sovereign God. God gives us His full attention, and He has full authority and unlimited power to answer our radical prayers for the hallowing of His name. As the late preacher E. V. Hill put it, we become subject to receiving at any moment the answer to our request.[2]

We may need to wait, possibly many years, for God's response. But the wonderful news is that we do not need to leave His presence while doing so. We understand that God knows what is best for us and does not make mistakes. Therefore, we acknowledge that His loving answer may be "no" or "not yet." These waiting times are difficult, but they are times of refining. They are times when we learn more of God Himself as we wait in His presence.

MY DAUGHTER SASHA

I met my daughter Sasha for the first time in the fall of 2002. She was nineteen years old and the mother of twins. Sasha's mother was a woman I had met in my years before coming to Christ—and while I was married to my first wife. (The story of our meeting is told in *Radical Redemption*.[3]) While I believe Sasha was genuinely interested in meeting me, I knew early on that her real desire was to meet my eldest son, Manny. Her mother had often spoken to her about her older brother. Growing up an only child, now as a young adult and mother herself, she very much wanted to know her half-sibling. Manny, however, was not yet ready to meet Sasha.

For the next thirteen years, Barbara and I prayed for two things. First, that Sasha would come to faith in Christ Jesus, and, second, that we would be able to have a Mill family reunion with all five of our children, their spouses, and our grandchildren present.

I recall spending an afternoon with Barbara trying to figure out how we could financially and logistically manage to get everyone together in one place since we were living in three states separated by thousands of miles. After my cabin experience of 2011, these were what I now called impossible prayer requests—impossible for human minds and hands to orchestrate or accomplish, and only possible with God's clear hand of provision. These are the kind of requests God delights in answering, for He alone gets all the glory. God would be glorified by bringing another sinner to saving faith and by bringing reconciliation to my family. He would truly be glorified and others would be given hope that what God would do for the Mills He could do for them.

A FAMILY COMES TOGETHER

By early 2015, through circumstances we could never have imagined, both Manny Jr. and his sister Cesia and their families had moved from Florida and were living close by us in Illinois. Although I accepted that a consequence of my sinful past was distant—and at times strained—relationships with my older children and grandchildren, I prayed for God to give me opportunities to build new relationships with them. In His rich mercy God first saw fit to call my daughter Cesia and her husband into church ministry, and led my son-in-law to study full time at Moody Bible Institute in Chicago. An exceedingly abundant blessing (Eph. 3:20) was being able to hold their first child, my sixth grandchild, just moments after his birth!

Cesia and Sasha have bonded as sisters over the years. Twice, Cesia traveled with me to New Jersey and was able to visit Sasha and her children. But Manny Jr. continued to be hesitant to meet, only exchanging occasional texts with her. That changed in March 2015, when Sasha decided to visit Illinois for the first time. Just three weeks after Manny and his family moved to Illinois, Sasha and the twins arrived for the weekend. Their visit coincided with our youngest son Kenneth's spring break, so everyone was present but our middle son, Howard. Without our planning, without our manipulation, God surprised us and brought our family together in our very own home!

Manny and Cesia shared with Sasha how it was only the grace of God, their heavenly Father, that enabled them to forgive me, their earthly father, for all the hurt and pain I had caused them and their mother. They told her that because they understood that they were forgiven in Christ Jesus and by Christ Jesus for their own sin, they were now able to forgive me. That Sunday, I cried tears of joy when, for the first time in thirty years, I attended church with my three oldest children, as well as all six of my grandchildren.

When Sasha returned home, she called a cousin to ask if she still attended church. The very next Sunday, Sasha began attending church with her. Seven weeks later, she was baptized. On the first Sunday in May 2015, Barbara and I sat at our kitchen table and watched a video recording of Sasha's baptism and heard her profession of faith in Christ Jesus as Savior. After thirteen years of asking, seeking, knocking, and waiting, our gracious heavenly Father said, "Yes."

AN AUDIENCE WITH THE KING

My beloved reader, let the truths of just a few of the many promises of Scripture sink deep into your heart and mind:

> The righteous cry out, and the Lord hears,
> and delivers them out of all their troubles.
> (Ps. 34:17)

Men have not heard nor perceived by the ear, nor has the eye seen any God besides You, who acts for the one who waits for Him. (Isa. 64:4)

I am the Lord your God, who brought you out of the land of Egypt; open your mouth wide, and I will fill it. (Ps. 81:10)

I am the vine, you are the branches. He who abides in Me, and I in him, bears much fruit; for without Me you can do nothing. If anyone does not abide in Me, he is cast out as a branch and is withered; and they gather them and throw them into the fire, and they are burned. If you abide in Me, and My words abide in you, you will ask what you desire, and it shall be done for you. By this My Father is glorified, that you bear much fruit; so you will be My disciples. (John 15:5–8)

For the eyes of the Lord are on the righteous, and His ears are open to their prayers; but the face of the Lord is against those who do evil. (1 Peter 3:12)

We have an audience with the King! We have His attention! We have His eye. We have His ear. What impossible prayer request do you have? What need do you have that the power of the Holy Spirit cannot supply? I urge you to take a radical time-out right now and begin asking, seeking, knocking, and waiting for God to respond. Do not turn away from Him and seek your answer in someone or something else. To do so is idolatry, because turning your face in another direction results in turning your back to God.

The writer to the Hebrews warns and instructs us, "Beware, brethren, lest there be in any of you an evil heart of unbelief in departing from the living God; but exhort one another daily, while it is called 'Today,' lest any of you be hardened through the deceitfulness of sin" (3:12–13).

God laid it on my heart to write this book as a strong exhortation, a call to my brothers and sisters in Christ to hallow His name through radical, biblical prayer. Because of the great grace I first received in my salvation and then again at the cabin in February 2011, I am now obligated to share with others that same grace in order to hallow God's holy name. It is my burning desire that the name of the Lord would be valued, cherished, adored, esteemed, and exalted by all people everywhere, including by you, beloved reader.

PHOTO BY JIM WHITMER PHOTOGRAPHY

Front row (from left): Justin Greaves, Isaiah Muñoz, Ethan Mill, Jordan Mill

Second row: Barbara and Manny Mill

Third row: Alyssa Greaves, Sasha Centeno, Cesia and Eli Muñoz, Adrian Mill, Manny and Loise Mill

Back row: Howard Mill, Kenneth Mill

———⁓———

A FRESH AND RADICAL REVIVAL

There are times in the Gospels when we see Jesus display righteous anger, and two of those times involve the misuse of the temple. John describes a cleansing that took place at the beginning of Jesus' ministry, while Matthew, Mark, and Luke describe a cleansing just prior to the crucifixion. In Mark 11:17, we read that

Jesus, after overturning the tables and chairs of the moneychangers, quoted the prophet Isaiah and said, "Is it not written, 'My house shall be called a house of prayer for all nations'? But you have made it a 'den of thieves.'"

While we do not have moneychangers in our churches today, I wonder: Would Jesus be pleased with the activities He finds there? Would He find our churches to be houses of prayer?

My dear reader, are you desperate to experience a fresh and radical revival in your heart that will illuminate your mind, convincing you that Jesus Christ is all-sufficient and all-satisfying? The times are urgent. Now is the time for you to take a radical time-out. Plead to God, your holy and loving heavenly Father, to baptize you afresh with the Holy Spirit. Fuel your prayers with the Word of God. Come before Him with a posture of surrender, an honest confession, a delight in His ownership, an attitude of expectancy, and an unwavering commitment to obedience—all for the hallowing of His holy name. *¡Aleluya!*

NOTES

Chapter 1: From Crisis to Conviction

1. C. H. Spurgeon, *Lectures to My Students: A Selection from Addresses Delivered to the Students of the Pastors' College, Metropolitan Tabernacle* (New York: Sheldon & Company, 1875), 40, from http://books.google.com.

2. E. M. Bounds, *The Complete Works of E.M. Bounds* (Radford, VA: Wilder Publications, 2008), 465.

Chapter 2: From Conviction to Radical Change

1. E. M. Bounds, *The Complete Works of E.M. Bounds* (Radford, VA: Wilder Publications, 2008), 449.

Chapter 4: Radical Prayer's Purpose

1. John Piper, "Be a Radically God-Centered Pastor," from www.desiringgod.org/conference-messages/be-a-radically-god-centered-pastor.

Chapter 5: Radical Prayer's Persistence

1. Tom Stuart, "One parable we all misinterpreted," Web blog post, November 26, 2010. Retrieved from tomstuart. org/2010/11/26/one-parable-we-all-misinterpreted/. Stuart is pastor and executive director of the Twin Cities House of Prayer in Minneapolis.

Chapter 6: Radical Prayer's Power

1. Spurgeon, *Lectures to My Students* (New York: Sheldon & Company, 1875), 79.

2. E. M. Bounds, *The Complete Works of E.M. Bounds* (Radford, VA: Wilder Publications, 2008), 365.

3. Ibid., 366.

Chapter 9: Radical Redemption

1. Arnold A. Dallimore, *George Whitefield: God's Anointed Servant in the Great Revival of the Eighteenth Century* (Wheaton, IL: Crossway, 1990), 200.

2. Ibid., 30.

3. Ibid.

4. As quoted in ibid., 201.

Chapter 10: Ready to Be Radical?

1. Spurgeon, *Lectures to My Students*, 79.

2. E. V. Hill, "What You Have When You Have Jesus," Founder's Week conference, Moody Bible Institute, February 1980.

3. Manny Mill with Jude Skallerup, *Radical Redemption* (Chicago: Moody, 2003), 164–168. Sasha had located me through the Internet, and Barbara and I met her in New Jersey one year after she called me.

ACKNOWLEDGMENTS

FIRST AND FOREMOST, I must acknowledge God, our holy and loving Father, for His radical grace that has empowered me to write this book alongside my dear wife Barbara and *Papito* (a Cuban term of endearment) Harold Smith.

Radical Prayer has been written for the radical hallowing of God my Father, who is no longer "simply" front and center in my life but now and forever my all and in all. And it is my radical prayer that He would become equally and wonderfully the same for all you who read this book.

There are many whose contributions to this book through the work of their hands and the witness of their lives have exhibited the super-duper, pure, loving, and irresistible grace of our mighty, surprising God! ¡*Aleluya!*

First and foremost is my wife, Barbara, the love of my life and my ministry and prayer partner. With a supernatural and fresh unction from the Holy Spirit, she miraculously interpreted and rearranged my creative "Spanglish" before sending the manuscript on to *Papito!*

Barbara, I must tell you that your God-given

strength and endurance to persevere no matter what, as well as your commitment to making this book simple yet profound—anchored in the highest level of biblical integrity—was a daily encouragement and motivation to me! Moreover, your high-level attention to detail pushed the both of us to produce a book that in my humble opinion is a "must-read" for anyone serious about taking their prayer life to radical levels. Barbarita, I am very thankful to God our Father for your unwavering desire, as well as *Papito*'s and mine, to make sure that every word in this book ultimately leads to the hallowing of God our Father's holy name. *¡Aleluya!*

To you, *Papito* Harold Smith, my deepest thanks for finding time to edit this book in between your busy role as President and CEO of *Christianity Today*. You are an amazing, unlimited fountain of encouragement to Barbara, our Radical Time Out (RTO) family, and to me! You and your dear wife Judy model radical, biblical prayer; and you have brought a wealth of biblical wisdom, discernment, and expertise to this project that has allowed us to complete this book triumphantly—and on time!

—⟡—

From the outset of this Spirit-led project, I have felt the strong desire—and the heavy burden—to find the right publishing partner. One with an extremely gifted team of godly people who would themselves be excited about a vision for bold, persistent, biblical, radical prayer.

God answered my own bold, persistent prayers by delivering Moody Publishers!

For starters, God clearly spoke with His distinct and unique voice to my amazing, longtime friend Greg Thornton, senior vice president of media at the Moody Bible Institute, on the matter of *Radical Prayer* being a book for Moody Publishers. Greg, I have cherished very much the times we met in your office to not only talk about my unique revival experience that prompted this book, but also to pray radically together for each other, our ministries, and the challenges we face. My prayer life has deepened as a result of those times together.

For Moody Publishers, my thanks to vice president Paul Santhouse, editorial director Randall Payleitner, and senior editor Jim Vincent. I am also grateful to publicity manager Janis Backing.

I must also thank God my holy Father for the immense army of people He has sent to bless me in countless ways over the recent past and most notably during the writing of this book.

Let me start with our Radical Time Out family led

by Nephtali Matta, Ministry Coordinator for Koinonia House® National Ministries (KHNM), and our social media consultant Jim Whitmer, together with his wife Mary. Thank you all for your radical focus on radical prayer and for the love you show our neighbors radically!

And thank you, Ken Cousins, for your radical obedience in responding to the Holy Spirit's prompting to ask me to join you in prayer for your son Jake and my son Kenneth, when we first met at the University of Pennsylvania in their freshman dorm room the fall of 2013. The Holy Spirit has rewarded your obedience by blessing dozens of fathers who join us every Wednesday at noon to radically intercede for hundreds of our sons and daughters.

Tom Horton, I cannot thank God our Father enough for you, my super-duper, bulletproof friend. You and your wife Wendy are always praying for me, my family and ministry, as we together take on the powers of hell in our unique Freedom God's Way weekends!

Dr. David Gieser, I must also thank God our Father for you. He used you mightily to invite me with persistence to come to CARBS (Christ-centered, Authentic, Relational, Build up, Strategic) on Saturday mornings at 6:30 a.m. Your invitation and consistent example of prayer has forever transformed my corporate prayer life. I am eternally indebted to you. At CARBS I have met so many mighty men of God who know how to pray radically and who have become my inseparable and forever prayer partners. Men like CARBS leader Scott Filline. Scott, you have become one of my most trusted friends. Your consistent leadership, driven by your love for all people, fires me up. And Jim Libby, your scholarship and Greek expertise helped me hallow our Father's name in a more precise way.

I must also thank God our Father for our KHNM board members who not only continuously model radical, biblical prayer but so generously granted Barbara and me the time to finish this book! I especially thank God for our three board officers: Joe Agnello, chair; Chuck Martin, secretary-treasurer; Don Leach, vice-chair; along with Kathy Woods (whose cabin in Wisconsin Barbara and I used to seclude ourselves to write this book), Pat Selvaggio, and Bob Wolfson (whose unique insight was very valuable to Barbara, *Papito*, and me), Bishop Ed Peecher, and Dr. Roger Haber.

I also thank God our Father for all of you whose stories appear in this book. You have provided the wondrous and God-honoring commentary that our biblical, radical prayers will be answered for the hallowing of God's name!

Let me close these acknowledgments with heartfelt thanks to God for His faithfulness to my precious family.

First, special thanks to my firstborn son, Manny Jr., for the insightful suggestions he (along with Nephtali) gave us to improve the book. I praise God for His bringing you and your family to live in Illinois, giving me the opportunity to develop deeper relationships with you, my daughter-in-law Loise, and grandsons Adrian, Jordan, and Ethan.

I praise God for giving daughter Cesia and her husband Eli the courage to leave the comforts of their life in Florida to obey your clear calling to come to Illinois to prepare for ministry. I could never have imagined that your first child, Isaiah, would be born here!

I am further humbled and grateful to our Father for His blessing and protection of our son Howard, who recently graduated from the University of Colorado, and was commissioned as a second lieutenant in the United States Marine Corps. And Kenneth, our youngest child, is now entering his junior year at the University of Pennsylvania—be strong in the Lord!

Last, but by no means least, our Father radically surprised Barbara and me as this book was in its final stages with our daughter Sasha's radical redemption. I look forward to seeing what God has in store for you, your husband Robert, and my grandchildren Justin and Alyssa. *¡Aleluya!*

Little wonder, then, that God, by His Spirit, and through the wonder of salvation found only in His Son, Jesus Christ, should have called me to write this book about radical prayer. He alone is worthy of our praise, honor, and glory. His name alone is to be hallowed.

—MANNY MILL

HOW TO CONTACT KOINONIA HOUSE

Mailing Address

Koinonia House® National Ministries

P.O. Box 1415

Wheaton, IL 60187-1417

Phone/Fax/Email

Phone: 630-221-9930

Fax: 630-221-9932

Email: info@khnm.net

Internet and Social Media

www.khnm.net

www.MannyMill.com

www.Facebook.com/

KoinoniaHouseNationalMinistries

www.instagram.com/koinonia_house

www.RadicalTimeOut.info

www.Twitter.com/MannyMill

THE RADICAL TESTIMONY OF MANNY MILL

In this candid and vividly personal book, Manny tells how his pursuit of pleasure led him to the depths of human despair. Manny's experiences will thrill you, his is faith will inspire you, and his words will challenge you to think about your life, your relationship with God, and your need for a radical redemption.

MOODY Publishers™

From the Word to Life

CLASSICS ON PRAYER

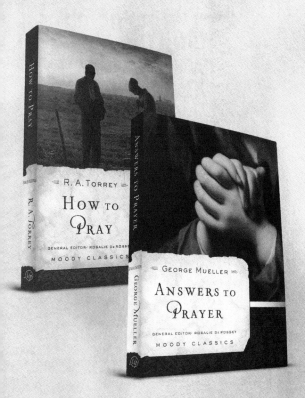

How to Pray outlines a practical strategy for living life in conversation with God. And through a narrative account, *Answers to Prayer* reveals how powerful and spiritually rewarding prayer can be.

MOODY
Publishers™

From the Word to Life

Where did I come from?
Why am I here?
Where am I going?

People have honest doubts and questions about God that deserve solid answers.

With doubters, seekers, and skeptics in mind, Pastor Ray Pritchard has updated this bestselling presentation of the gospel in a clear, straightforward way using simple language and clear Scripture references.